Buddhist Dzogchen

Being Happiness Itself

David Paul Boaz

Waterside Productions

Printed in the United States of America

First Printing, 2021

ISBN-13: 978-1-951805-43-2 print edition
ISBN-13: 978-1-951805-44-9 ebook edition

Waterside Productions
2055 Oxford Ave
Cardiff, CA 92007
www.waterside.com

For
David Antonio Pacheco
and
Gianna Nicole Pacheco
from whom
I have learned so much.

Table of Contents

Preface: Light from The County Jail

Notes from Students of David Paul Boaz

Dear Dr. Boaz,

"Your lecture 'The Good News About Suicidal Ideation' literally saved my life. I know now that God has given me a precious gift. I pray that I will figure out how to use it…"

"Thank you for your book and the meditation practices and inspired teaching I have received from you…You have helped me to free myself of serious obstructions to my thinking that for many years have caused me and my family great emotional pain."

"I wanted to let you know how your mindfulness of breathing meditation and the mantra prayer have helped me to get off psych meds and sleep better… (This) mantra of inner peace is in my mind day and night…I 'Let it be as it is'…Thank you for the Jesus picture."

Thank you for giving us the Buddhist Refuge. I am, per your request leading our meditation meetings every morning. I read aloud from your book. There are 18 of us practicing here in F4. F6, D2, and E4 have about the same…We bow to one another…We all have the Dalai Lama picture in our cells…We miss your humor, and the guided meditations…"

"Using your secular (I'm not into religion) mindfulness practice instructions I have actually learned to cultivate a peaceful, sometimes happy mind…My panic attacks and anger problems are a thing of the past (almost)…I am sharing your course with my family."

"Your humorous responses to my inane questions have allowed me to see that the 'prodigious drama of your life' should not be taken too seriously. You said, 'See it all as a divine comedy'...So 'I' am not the center of the universe after all. What a relief!"

"Thank you so much...You have taught me that Jesus and Buddha both came to earth to save us from the sin of ignoring our own *inner* Christ Nature...I know I am not an awful (person)...I am Presence of God!...This has forever changed my life for the better."

"The teaching you have given me is priceless, light and simple to apply in my life...My quiet mind presence is quickly found and the result is to me a very personal feeling of peace and gratitude for, as you often say 'the great gift of your life just as it is now'."

"If God forbids killing that means it's a sin to kill yourself...I tried it three times already...God gave me my life. So I can't take it away...I believe that (now)."

"The teaching of the Buddha that you have given us feels so familiar, as if it is a constant reminder of who I am...this Presence!...It's all so clear and obvious...Thank you!"

"Thank you for presenting your 'Awareness Management' strategy to our staff...We use your mindfulness handout with our patients in the PAC (Psychiatric Acute Care). The mindfulness practice has proven to be of considerable benefit for those with anxiety and sleep disorder, which are all too prevalent here...We very much appreciate your effort..."

Your mind training work with our PAC inmates has been exemplary...I appreciate your practical knowledge of General Psychiatry in a 'spiritual' context; not to mention your irreverent but not irrelevant humor...'Keep 'em laughing'...Thank you for your commitment to us...Thanks for the Jesus and Buddha photos, and all the books for our library."

"Joey—in PAC-1 is having a very bad day. Please see him on your rounds." —Chaplain

"I hope that your Tibetan is better than your Sanskrit! Let me help you with the latter...That said, your teaching has prepared me to take Refuge with the Tibetan Lama who visits here … You have helped me to understand that my intellectual arrogance is a rather nasty form of ignorance … Thank you for your guidance on this prickly path to wisdom."

"Your advice to see everyone as Buddha has helped me from being so insanely judgmental … Does that mean I am Buddha too? … Thank you for the awareness of all this …"

"After many years of (sleep disorder) I am sleeping normally thanks to the 'practice of the night' that you teach … I am willingly sharing it with others in the POD … Thank you …"

"After years of misery and hatred and mental breakdowns I have 'surrendered' as you call it, everything to my spiritual practice … It is the most valuable and important thing in my life … Your teaching has saved my life! … *OM AH HUM* … I want to meet *your* Lama …"

"I feel my connection to mother earth and the whole cosmos … I don't feel separate anymore … Strange peace … I practice bodhicitta for my fellow inmates … Ironic that I am given jail to meet you and change my life … In mantra prayer I feel my *Diné* roots … Everything is so bright … I feel your presence often, especially in *inipi*. I always will."

I am incredibly thankful for your introduction to me of the Buddha Presence that I am. It has changed everything for me …'Who am I? That I Am!' You have taught me *that*."

"My mantra prayer goes on almost by itself, without trying … Walking meditation has been my saving grace because I cannot sit for long without (anxiety) … I am peaceful for the first time in my life, even in the din of this hellish place … Someday I will teach this."

Your book and guided meditations are a Godsend! Thank you my *Kalyanamitta* for mirroring to me my own happiness, 'always already present in this very moment now'. So I stay present to it instead of suffering over something I can't control, which is just about everything … When I forget I come back to my mantra breath. It's everything I need."

"The light of your selfless Buddha mind makes my own teaching, such as it is, real…I remain present to the luminous mind-stream of His Holiness, and of Lord Buddha through your kind, and not always so subtle wisdom counsel…I very much miss our talks and your guided meditation…You are always with me. *Lama Khyen, Lama Khyen.*"

Introduction: Being Happy Now

Our fundamental innate mind of clear light. The Buddha told, "Mind is not mind; the nature of mind is clear light". That is the primordial wisdom mind founding principle of Buddhist *Dzogchen* view, practice, and result/fruition that for 2000 years has been known as the Great Perfection—the Great Completion of our various human strategies for deep inner peace and profound relative, and even ultimate happiness.

Nice ornamental concept. We shall in these pages move beyond habitual dependence upon our biased concepts and beliefs to an innermost *direct experience* of the indwelling always already present fearless sky-like Presence of the *Perfect Sphere of Dzogchen*. We shall remain present to what it is that Buddhism in general, and *Dzogchen* in particular, are actually good for.

How does opening our heart-mind to receive the *direct transmission* of *Dzogchen* selfless boundless love and wisdom enhance our present human happiness, right here now? How does such an imperfect surrender of self lessen our afflictive emotions—fear/anxiety, anger, hatred, blame, grief, guilt, greed, envy, and pride—without altogether "spiritually bypassing" our emotional nature? How may we experience such destructive emotions without suppressing them, or being individually and collectively consumed, and defined by them? Do we really require years of Buddhist practice to experience such a selfless happiness mind state that is already present within us? So many questions.

You Dear Reader—whether you are a beginning or intermediate yogi/yogini, or just "thinking about it", shall herein enhance your present wisdom through new and perhaps deeper innermost wisdom answers—your own answers—already present within you now.

There is no need to *believe* any of this. Concepts and beliefs *about* emotional-spiritual happiness have very little to do with the process of awakening (*bodhi*) to who it is that you actually are—your selfless "supreme identity"—indwelling, intimate bright Presence of That. The direct experience of your Buddha nature is more powerful than concept-belief.

We shall consider together that this timeless, selfless enlightened identity is, wonder of wonders, "already accomplished from the very beginning"—always present and fully embodied deep within the human body and mind. *Realizing That, everything is realized*. We shall see that is the way that things in this interdependent world of spacetime phenomena actually exist. That is the *Dzogchen* "non-meditation" of all-embracing primordial *kosmos* itself. We shall learn to align our body and mind with the truth of That.

Well, just what is this rather paradoxical "non-meditation"? That is the very theme of this little book. Yet, we may say for now that it is a direct result of the continuity of the whole of your patient, compassionate lifeworld love-wisdom practice—where you *choose* to place your awareness at any given moment. Love and wisdom heal fear and anger.

The bright silent stillness of your Buddha mind—bright Presence of That—here in the midst of all this distraction is an immediate aperture, *a finite portal into infinite reality itself*, vast original ground of Buddha nature of mind. This infinite Presence of the ground, the finite distractions, the awareness portal, and the infinite ground itself always already abide in a relationship of identity, sameness, non-difference, in a word, nondual cognition.

Please consider this: your awakening process is not an enlightenment of a self-ego-I; not a process of realizing a smarter, more cool version of yourself; not a process of control by the will. It is rather, a process of seeing and knowing the prior and always present identity and unity of ego-I with primordial *buddic* love/compassion and

wisdom. It's showing up and being present here and now to your practice—always in the face of fear and doubt—with a bit of clarity and
bliss added in as a motivator. And every thought, feeling, intention,
and action of yours is embraced in this precious practice, just as it is.

Therefore, awakening (*bodhi*) is letting be this luminous continuum of clear light pristine "naked awareness", this boundless inclusion of self in selfless primordial ground of being—that vast whole
of reality itself—beyond yet including the body and concept-mind.
So, "leave it alone and let it be as it is". Indeed, this is the trans-
conceptual, nondual (union of perceiving subject and its objects)
unity of *Dzogchen* view, practice, and fruition.

Dzogchen is considered by those who know to be a radically simple, yet very difficult direct and expedited path to "full *bodhi*" real-
ization/awakening of Gautama the Buddha's nondual primordial
love-wisdom mind—our very Buddha nature of mind. This realization is the primary cause of both relative conventional happiness,
and the wondrous potential of enlightenment, liberating ultimate
human happiness—Happiness Itself.

Yet, a bit paradoxically to concept-mind, such ultimate enlightenment is not at all the goal of the *Dzogchen* path. The *goal* of
spiritual practice is always the practice of the Path itself, here and
now, moment to moment *connection* to your innermost Buddha
mind, "Big Mind"—bright Presence of That—in all your arising
thoughts, feelings, and actions ("Small Mind"). That is your immediate happiness now! How shall you do this?

It is from this gradual recognition that spontaneously arises
human altruistic *bodhicitta*—the thought, intention and action for
the benefit of living beings. And That—on the accord of the masters and sages of the entire primordial love-wisdom Great Tradition
of our species—is the lifeworld result, the actual fruition of our
relative everyday happiness; and in due course and by grace, of ultimate happiness that is enlightenment, and liberation from earth-
bound human suffering. This is the profound teaching of Gautama
Shakyamuni the Buddha of this present age. An ambitious program, to be sure.

My intention and my hope is that this little book will provide a non-scholarly introduction to what is often considered the subtlest and highest teaching of the Buddha so that you, Dear Reader, may receive the immeasurable and immediate benefit—happy peace of mind—not later, after years of "advanced practice", but in your present busy life just as it is now. *Buddic* pie in the sky? It depends upon the expanse of your view.

I pray that you will let this powerful, peaceful preparatory *Dzogchen* mindfulness teaching of the Buddha be an opening into recognition, then stable realization of your indwelling already present luminous Presence of the boundless whole of reality itself that is the *Perfect Sphere of Dzogchen*—the "natural state" of the mind that is always present now.

We are told that this boundless, all-embracing formless, empty *dharmakaya* whole has an immediate imprint, aspect or Presence in the human being arising within it. To conceptualize it, call it formless, timeless innate clear light love-wisdom Buddha mind that abides now within your heart of hearts—by whatever name, concept, or belief. That after all is the primordial Buddha nature that you are now. And that is the Buddha's teaching for the ages, essentialized for you in the nondual teaching of the Great Perfection.

All the avatars, masters and *mahasiddha's* who have come to earth to lighten the burden of our suffering have told it: Our "supreme identity" is the immediacy of innermost love-wisdom Presence. Who is it that I am? That I Am! That is the I AM Presence of all the Buddha's (awakened beings), and of Moses and the Prophets, and of Jesus the Christ.

That is the resolution of the otherwise unanswerable metaphysical question, "Who Am I?" That "I Am Presence" remains after the personal "I am" of self-ego-I is placed for a time in non-conceptual mindful *shamatha* meditative abeyance. Then, this ultimately apparitional self sense is examined through analytical penetrating insight known as *vipashyana* meditation. The union of these two—*shamatha* and *vipashyana*—reveals the true selfless identity of the troubled self. We shall see that in no-self (*anatman*) acting in the relative world for the benefit of living beings abides your own ultimate human happiness.

Thus do we approach the Great Perfection through beginning *shamatha* mindfulness. We practice the contemplative dissolution of limited mind ego-I into the primordial awareness-consciousness ground of all-embracing, all-pervading *Perfect Sphere of Dzogchen* while still ambulating in the hectic world of spacetime form. This ultimate formless awareness of the boundless whole of reality itself is the pristine selfless Buddha nature of your very own mind. And it pervades the mindstream of all beings.

But wait! What if my present "global web of belief" knows of no such "innermost Presence". What evidence do I have of this occult and spooky "Presence"? To be sure, such evidence is "trans-empirical", trans-conceptual and directly experiential. Like Great Love itself, "innermost secret" Presence of the clear light primordial ground admits of no purely objective "proof". It awaits recognition in inner silence beyond habitually thinking concept-mind. Thus do we expand our cognitive horizons from mere *objective*, often negative, worrisome self-centered thinking and ruminating—into our subtle *subjective* cognitive dimension. We shall herein deepen our knowledge and practice of That.

The awareness-consciousness processional of our human cognition has at least four dimensions of experience: 1) pre-conceptual ordinary direct perception, just prior to conceptual imputation and naming; 2) outer exoteric objective conceptual experience where we spend nearly all of our waking lives; 3) inner esoteric subjective contemplative experience that unveils our inner spiritual life; and 4) perfectly subjective "innermost secret" nondual experience—all-embracing dimension of the *Perfect Sphere of Dzogchen*.

The third and fourth of these cognitive dimensions necessarily remain inaccessible to the contemplatively untrained human mind brimming with its naive cognitive biases. Such a mind limits the causes of suffering to state/stages one and two—external circumstance. You shall discover, if you have not already done so, that contemplative yogic practice makes the subtle realms three and four accessible, useful, even blissful.

The Buddha termed our ignorance of this subjective inner and "innermost secret" dimensional experience—not surprisingly—"ignorance" (*avidya, marigpa*). Jesus the Christ referred to it as sin (*hamartia*), literally "missing the mark" of the great nondual truth of the matter. Such ignorance is, on the accord of both of these sublime masters, the primary cause of human suffering. Suffering is the *activity* of desire/attachment/clinging to the inherently impermanent (*anitya*) stuff of the world. We'll see in these pages that the Buddha has offered for our consideration some surprising choices as to how to free ourselves from such ignorance, and the suffering it causes, that we may be happy now.

Please remember the following pithy logical truth when considering subtle wisdom phenomena: *Absence of evidence is not evidence of absence.* The absence of objective evidence of such subjective interior phenomena as "innermost Buddha love-wisdom mind Presence" does not constitute evidence of absence of such subjective primordial wisdom truths of our great Primordial Wisdom Tradition. That it does is the result of ignorance—illogical conceptual cognitive bias against presently hidden dimensions three and four above—the inherently false dominant trope of our hyper-rational "common sense" egoistic thinking.

Such enhanced wisdom reasoning is known to the wise as the mythopoetic "logic of the non-conceptual". It transcends, yet embraces the intrinsically binary, dualistic true-false structure of the semiotics (logical syntax, semantic meaning, factual pragmatics) of our obsessive linguistic conceptual thinking and discourse.

Well, if *Dzogchen* is so simple, why is it difficult? Because in order to awaken the human heart-mind to our indwelling always already present clear light Buddha nature, or Christ nature, we must first train the obsessively conceptual, narcissistic "wild horse of the mind" in the quiescent peace of trans-conceptual mindful *shamatha* meditation. This requires some mental self-discipline, patience, and a bunch of courage. How is this so?

As we know all too well, our self-ego-I is inherently fraught with anxiety and resistance to most cognitive processes that will cause psychological emotional change/growth beyond our present uncomfortable comfort zones. Self has prodigious conceptual "ego defense mechanisms"—cognitive biases—mostly unconscious, that protect it from such scary change. It's easier to remain bound in habitual thinking. This is true even of disciplined meditation practitioners, as well as those with highly developed intellects. It is particularly true of those fortunate folks who possess both of these qualities.

A kind, secure, intelligent, fluent and loosely held ego is required to reflexively deconstruct its own self-destructive defenses and biases. And that takes courage, patience/tolerance, and an honest character—the all too rare qualities that allow us to see clearly that much of our unhappiness and emotional suffering are the result, not of the actions of others, but of our own negative thought, intention and action.

Further, character requires the qualities of kindness and generosity, virtue and ethical discipline, diligence and effort, and wise discernment. These are prerequisites for approach to the Buddhist *Dzogchen* Path. So, *Dzogchen* is for those who have already developed good character. These qualities of character are in no way transcendental, but are attributes of a relative conventional self-ego-I acting in the cause and effect world of relative spacetime existence. And these qualities of character develop gradually within the embrace of meditation practice—immediate connection to compassionate *buddic* Presence.

Therefore, beginning and intermediate Buddhist practice does not advocate, nor does it require the total transcendence, much less the denigration of self-ego-I. Buddha told that we lift self into the no-self love-wisdom of our selfless Buddha nature/Buddha mind. *"No-self is the true refuge of self"*. Indeed, without our sense of self who is it that *chooses* to establish a dharma practice in the first place? Who is it that chooses to benefit others? Who is it that experiences the peace and "yogi's bliss" of sustained selfless practice?

Please consider the following essential primordial wisdom principle of happiness. *Both human happiness and unhappiness are the immediate result of where we* choose *to place our attention—our awareness—at any given moment! Clear as a bell. But how do we do this?*

How indeed. You now already know. Yes. We *choose* to tame and train the "wild horse of the mind" in conscious "placement of awareness/attention" upon our always present innermost Buddha mind Presence. Inevitable human adversity still arises, albeit less than before, but we now have a choice as to how to *respond* to it—with fear, anxiety and anger, or with fearless, skillful grace. Thus is human happiness in no small part what I have come to call *awareness management.* We shall learn in these pages to manage our moment to moment mind-stream of both common and uncommon awareness.

And yes, to accomplish such presence of mind we must first learn basic *shamatha*—quiescent mindfulness practice—mindful breathing with peaceful mantra prayer—our constant connection to Presence. As we begin to understand what is required to be free and deeply happy now, we either continue our practice, or we do not. There is no magic pill. And this requires intelligence, self discipline, and courage. Simple, but not so easy.

Thus it is, nondual *Dzogchen Ati Yoga* works through immediate, non-conceptual *direct yogic experience* with our already present Buddha mind, open "instant Presence" of clear light wisdom mind *rigpa*—prior to conceptual ego defenses of our present "global web of belief"; prior to heady dualistic Buddhist dialectics; prior to the pernicious subject-object split—just prior to doubt, and judgment, good or bad, of this endless arising continuum of phenomenal appearances. We learn to "let it be as it is" (*Wu-Wei*).

Just so, it is our nondual primordial awareness essential Buddha nature of mind—the nondual state of undistracted moment to moment "non-meditation" as primordial Presence that is at first "directly introduced", non-conceptually, to the prepared aspirant by the *Dzogchen* master. This does not mean that we "turn over" our lives to an outer Guru. Far from it. Rather, our outer spiritual mentor mirrors to us our own already present "innermost secret" Guru, indwelling always at the spiritual Heart (*hridaym*).

This then enhances our preliminary *Dzogchen* meditation practices—*shamatha, vipashyana, ngöndro*. Indeed, it adorns with clarity all of our worldly thought and activity. After all, meditation practice is the totality of all of our thought, intention, and action.

It is that numinous, luminous, timeless natural and pristine primordial awareness—beyond our concepts and beliefs *about* it—in which we learn to settle, then rest, even in the midst of all kinds of positive and negative lifeworld distractions. It is that nondual yogic direct perception (*yogi pratyaksa*) through which we gently tame and lovingly train the unruly mind of self-ego-I.

Quiescent mindfulness meditation is the "first step of this journey of a thousand miles" (Lao Tzu). Meanwhile, as Buddha told, "Let it be as it is and rest your weary mind; all things are perfect exactly as they are". This is the perfect nondual view of *Dzogchen*.

So now, with your open Zen Mind/Beginner's Mind at the ready, and your cognitive biases wisely placed in abeyance, let us now engage the meditation practices of the Buddha that are the very foundation of wondrous *Ati Dzogchen* view and practice.

Buddhist Meditation: *Shamatha* and *Vipashyana*

> The nature of mind is the unity of awareness and emptiness.
> The nature of mind is clear light.
>
> —Gautama the Buddha

Buddhist Meditation is the necessary means and method for awakening to, and compassionate expression of our always present indwelling love-wisdom Buddha mind (*buddhadhatu, buddhajnana*)—subtle numinous Presence of That—by whatever name or concept. Buddhist meditation practice—yogic mind training—has two voices, *shamatha* quiescent mindfulness, and *vipashyana* analytic penetrating insight. Both are imperative to engaging and completing the Buddhist path, as well to approaching the *Dzogchen* path.

For 25 centuries Buddhist philosophy and practice has changed, and been changed by every cultural tradition it has entered. For example, as Indian Buddhism entered China its spacious *shunyata/* emptiness metaphysical foundation came to be seen and experienced through the natural earthy fullness of Chinese Taoist (Daoist) philosophy and practice.

Here the Indian Buddhist primordial emptiness of self and its experienced phenomenal world became *The Way* or Path of Tao, the natural order of the *kosmos* itself. In contradistinction to Indian Buddhist dialectics, conceptual speculation and orthodoxy were resisted in Taoism. The propitious result of this metaphysical mergence became Mahayana Ch'an Buddhism, then Zen Buddhism upon entering Japan. In Japanese Zen meditation (*zazen*) the practice is *shikantaza* (*shamatha*, "just sitting").

Just so, Indian Buddhism was changed as it entered Tibet with Padmasambhava in the 8th century and merged with the indigenous Bön tradition, which already contained the very nondual view and practice we know as *Ati Dzogchen* (*Appendix B*).

In the 20th century Indian Mahayana and Tibetan Vajrayana (Tantrayana/Mantrayana) Buddhism became firmly established in the West—in Europe and in the United States. Once again Indian and Chinese Buddhism have both changed and been changed by Western mind and culture. The efflorescence in the West of non-objectivist, non-conceptual, nondual view and practice of esoteric Buddhism have tamed some of the cognitive excesses of our prevailing cultural metaphysic that is monolithic, monistic Metaphysical Scientific Materialism/Physicalism.

Meanwhile, the wanton materialism and consumerism (Ken Wilber's "Boomeritis") that has colonized the Western heart and mind—along with its pseudo-scientific empirical hyper-objective habit of mind—has trespassed the nondual primordial purity of Indian and Tibetan Buddhist meditation systems as they have evolved through the Four Tenet Systems (Boaz 2020) to become the teaching pinnacle that is *Ati Dzogchen* and Essence *Mahamudra* view and praxis (*Ch. 2 below*).

My reflections on Buddhist meditation herein represent an imperfect attempt to balance this prodigious coming to meet of the complementary wisdom mind-streams of the subjective wisdom of the East, and the objective wisdom of the West. "O East is East and West is West, and *ever* the twain shall meet" (apologies to Kipling).

What Is Meditation?

Meditation is a simple non-conceptual but conscious cognitive activity that opens a finite human awareness portal into the infinite vast expanse of all embracing primordial awareness-consciousness being itself in whom we arise and participate.

This fecund *kosmic* consciousness womb is the unbounded unbroken whole in which, or in whom meditator, and everything else that arises in spacetime as our experience is embraced and included. It is this infinite order of timeless, formless, all-pervading *ultimate* realty that enfolds *relative* finite spacetime reality as it continuously unfolds, arises, participates, and is thereby instantiated—including all of us.

Thus is finite meditation our instant and continuous *connection* to that nondual infinite whole. This is more or less the nondual Primordial Wisdom view as it has arisen in the cognitive history of our species.

Meditation (*dhyana/jhana, Ch'an/Zen, bhavana*) literally means *cultivation* or development of inner peace and equanimity, altruistic compassion, and skillful luminous wisdom for the benefit of living beings. How? Through *contemplation* of, or meditating upon the primordial ground of being, by whatever name or concept. Luminous, numinous Presence of That.

Non-conceptual, nondual *samadhi* (*sam*/perfect, *dhi*/wisdom mind) is the *ultimate* result of *relative* yogic (yoking, union) meditation practice. *Dhyana/samadhi* is the final state/stage of the Buddha's Eightfold Path (*Pali Canon*) to perfect wisdom; and the 6th of the Six *Paramitas*/Perfections of the Mahayana Path.

Meditation is "self-regulation" mind training as focused attention and awareness which moves the practitioner from thinking discursive cognition to trans-conceptual contemplative cognition, where abide peaceful, lucid, compassionate, blissful mind states.

We shall soon see that mindfulness (calm abiding, *shamatha, sati*)—Buddha's "mindfulness of breathing (*anapanasati*)—is the invariant ingredient in all systems of meditation, whether secular or religious/spiritual.

By virtue of our indivisible prior and always present love-wisdom mind unity of inclusion in that vast whole, there abides herein a bright, numinous *Presence* (*vidya, rigpa, Christos*) of this primordial reality ground—by whatever name or conceptually contrived concept—necessarily always already present at the spiritual Heart (*hridaym*) of the participant, whether in a meditative "state of Presence", or in a conceptual state of distraction. It is this prodigious practice of mindful meditation that awakens the practitioner to the nondual (subject-object unity) innermost truth of our being here in time.

In other words, the practice of meditation offers a finite cognitive link or connection to the prior, infinite primordial awareness-consciousness ground that is the indivisible unity of we finite participating parts with the infinite, all inclusive whole itself.

The short term, and long term experiential result of such contemplative practice is an emotional sense of peace, well being, and connectedness, even bliss—which is life-changing as it becomes integrated into our lifeworld of relative space and time.

Who Is It That Meditates?

While it is the self-ego-I who *chooses* to establish a meditation practice, and who chooses the *placement of attention/awareness* upon the object of meditation—the breath, or emptinesss/buddha nature— it is our basal, primordial love-wisdom Buddha mind itself that meditates us. The mind of self-ego-I, Suzuki Roshi's "Small Mind", is already included and embraced by primordial emptiness of Buddha mind/wisdom mind—"Big Mind". It is this vast aboriginal mind or ground that assimilates the physical, perceptual, mental, and emotional raw data of experience, then wondrously organizes it all into nonjudgmental, non-conceptual, nondual "primordially present" love and wisdom—in short, our always present love-wisdom mind—bright Presence of That. We learn through meditation practice to settle into, gently rest in, and then spontaneously express in love-wisdom conduct that pristine primordial Buddha nature of mind (*buddhadhatu, buddhajnana*).

It is *relative*, conventional mindful mantra prayer, upon the life-giving *prana/spirit wind* of the breath, that connects to *ultimate* meaning (Ultimate Truth) which embraces *relative* meaning (Relative Truth) in the whole of this contemplative process. This post-conceptual, dualistic relative Small Mind stabilizing process reflexively refers beyond itself to nondual, all embracing ultimate Big Mind which necessarily embraces and includes it. Such a penetrating unifying process demonstrates the mythopoetic nondual "logic of the non-conceptual" which transcends and includes our dualistic discursive mind (Klein 2006).

As the hyper-judgmental "wild horse" of conceptual mind simmers down and rests in wisdom mind Presence of the very primordial Buddha *nature of mind*, already present love-wisdom arises as peaceful loving kindness and ethical conduct toward all living beings—including oneself. In the Buddhist Mahayana tradition such altruistic compassionate thought, intention, and action for the benefit of human and other living beings—including our Mother Earth—is known as *bodhicitta*.

No small matter is at stake in our consideration of the what and the who of meditation. All the buddhas (awakened beings), sages, and *mahasiddhas* have told it: the loving-kindness expression of altruistic *bodhicitta* is the real cause of human happiness.

Indeed, by the lights of some recent postmodern cultural anthropology, it was not survival of the fittest, but survival of the kindest—Late Paleolithic Homo proto-altruism—that is the primary cause of the rise and success of the otherwise unexceptional species *H. sapiens*, the only extant species of the genus Homo.

So, we learn to counter our harsh judgments of self and others with loving kindness; we accept whatever arises in Small Mind—the senses, concepts, and feelings—exactly as it is. No need to try to change anything. No need to fix anything. No need to try to stop thinking; nor to try to accomplish "positive thinking". Simply witness, without evaluation, your thoughts and feelings as they come and go. Witness this display of the mind with gentle loving compassion, like a mother watches her child at play.

Meta-cognitively, reflexively be aware of your awareness in this moment now. No need to change or censor any of it. No need to grasp at or reject or react to any of it. Thoughts are merely thoughts. Thoughts cannot harm us. They need not become harmful negative emotions. Thoughts possess only the power that we *choose* to bestow upon them. It's all the magical display of the mind. No need to like or dislike your experience. All that arises in the mind is utterly natural. Easier said than done.

And because the primordial ground of the mind—*The Perfect Sphere of Dzogchen, dharmakaya*—is utterly untainted by negative thought and emotion, just so, the contents of mind arising therein are "primordially pure" in their ultimate nature, albeit not quite so pure from the relative view. The mind and all its stuff are always a prior and present unity with its perfectly subjective primordial source/ground. No problem at all.

So, please don't take your scattered "monkey mind", your "wild horse of the mind" too seriously. The adventitious negative afflictions of the mind—*Aversion*: fear, anger, hostility, hatred, regret/guilt; and *Attraction/Attachment*: raging sense desire, greed, pride, jealousy/envy—all may, through practice, be lifted and released via our love-wisdom mind connection. That is the gift of Presence inherent in contemplative mindfulness practice. It's a *choice* of the judicious placement of attention/awareness. There's plenty of self-effacing humor here. Discover it, laugh with yourself, rest and be happy.

The Buddha told it well, "Let it be as it is and rest your weary mind, all things are perfect exactly as they are". Your *ultimate* Buddha mind/wisdom mind Presence already knows this. Let us learn to connect to it through our *relative* imperfect meditation practice. Peace of mind and *bodhicitta* compassion is the wondrous result.

It is through this radical skillful "right understanding" and self-acceptance that meditation effects its miraculous result. Such nondual wisdom cannot be told in words. Wisdom mind experiences it directly through *feeling* awareness—this "peace that passes all understanding". So, we simply practice—mindfulness and mantra—opening to receive that lucent already present Presence—without expecting anything at all. Who am I? All the avatars who have incarnated into earth time have told it: living Presence of That I Am!

Therefore, your primary responsibility is *awareness management.* So, right now be reflexively meta-cognitively aware of your present awareness. As compassionate, non-judging witness Presence, monitor whatever arises in the mind—sights, sounds, smells, your breath, feelings of love, sense desire, anger, thinking, guilt and past regret, worry about the future, present mood states, anxiety, impatience, gratitude. There's plenty to worry about. And lots to be happy about. From the view of your loving Buddha mind, observe the whole show—without evaluating or judging any of it. That is the View. That is the Meditation. So, settle in upon the mindful breath, with a mantra if you have one (e.g. *OM AH HUM*) and rest in the already present Presence of your Buddha nature/Buddha mind. Do it now for two minutes. Relax into it and enjoy. Go ahead and do it now.

Your psychological attitude now is *shoshin*—Zen Mind/ Beginner's Mind—placing in abeyance questions, judgments, the grasping/attachment and aversion/avoidance that is the constant activity of the busy mind of your self-ego-I. Enjoy your open awareness with a minimum of self-identification. Such "open monitoring meditation" is the first step of *shamatha*, "focused attention meditation". Who is it that meditates? It is your Big Mind love-wisdom mind—clear light now present Presence of That.

Shamatha (*sati, smriti, bhavana*)—calm abiding—may be seen as the foundation of Buddhist contemplative and ethical practice. *Shamatha* literally means calm or quiescent abiding. It is the Buddhist antidote to the distracting mind states of *excitation* or obsessive sensory desire and stimulation, and *laxity* or failure of focused attention on the breath, or Buddha Presence, or emptiness, or other object of meditation.

By cultivating quiescent, non-conceptual *shamatha* or "calm abiding" we utilize the breath, or other meditation object, to settle the "wild horse of the mind" into, and then rest in clear peace of the vast expanse of spacious, boundless emptiness/*shunyata*—the very nature of *dharmakaya*—nonlocal, nondual whole of always present Buddha nature of mind.

Shamatha

Shamatha is, as Buddha told, "mindfulness of breathing"—the gentle *placement of awareness-attention* upon the movement of the breath in the belly; the *feeling* of the breath, over and above mere *thinking* about it. Meditation is not a higher form of thinking. Wisdom mind Presence is not a "higher self" upgrade of our habitually thinking self-ego-I. Contemplative practice is mostly trans-rational, non-conceptual, nonlocal, even nondual, beyond the destructive duality or separation of knowing subject and its objects known. As quantum pioneer Werner Heisenberg told, "The separation between subject and object does not exist. Subject and object are only one".

Quiescent mindfulness develops focused attentional stability and a bright vivid acuity of the mind upon its contemplative object—the movement of the breath, emptiness/Buddha nature/ Buddha mind, or an image of the Buddha, or tantric meditation deity, or for Christians, the luminous indwelling heartfelt Presence of the Christ. After all, That is who we actually are!

Indeed, Lord Buddha, by his own account, accomplished his final *bodhi* mind love-wisdom mind awakening through engaging the mantra seed syllable *OM* while abiding in undistracted, selfless "mindfulness of breathing" (*Appendix A*).

"Mindfulness of breathing" (*anapanasati*) is then the skillful method or means for accomplishing *shamatha* or meditative quiescence. Moreover, on the accord of Buddhist scholar-practitioner B. Alan Wallace (2007):

> Mindfulness ... must be accompanied by the mental faculty of introspection ... the function of monitoring the meditative process ... a type of metacognition ... in the development of *shamatha*, swiftly detecting the occurrence of either excitation or laxity.

As subtle introspective awareness detects that the mind has wandered from its object of meditation, through one or another thinking/feeling distraction, attentional awareness is immediately returned to the peaceful quiescent breath—again, and again.

The practitioner gradually "progresses" through the nine stages of *shamatha*. Its ultimate accomplishment leaves only *samadhi*, nondual pure awareness, luminosity, and bliss. Thoughts continue to arise but "self-liberate" at or near the instant of their arising, leaving no karmic imprint.

So, as *shamatha* evolves through its nine stages—the final stage being nondual *samadhi*—the mind is now prepared to "rest in its natural state", the wisdom of emptiness, *Perfect Sphere of Dzogchen*, free of conventional realities and of attentional objects of meditational support, for example the breath, or mantra, or image presence of a deity. Meanwhile, use the supports.

Potential distractions arise as before, and pass away as they will, without intervention, introspection, judgment or antidote. The mind rests in the always already present purity of its own nonlocal, nondual natural state of original primordial awareness-consciousness itself, the very Buddha nature of mind. The result is peaceful bliss. But, in the meantime, remain close to the breath, and get a mantra (e.g. *OM AH HUM*). The mind that is filled with the light and vibrational sound of mantra has no remaining space for afflictive thoughts and emotions.

That all said, most of this "no-self help" is mere idealized concepts and beliefs *about* meditation, until one enters into it by establishing an effective practice. Let a qualified teacher help you establish your practice, then introduce you to a qualified *Dzogchen* meditation master, and a like-minded *sangha* community.

An effective meditation practice cannot be learned from a book, not even this one, nor from a DVD series by a famous spiritual person. Still, books and tapes by Buddhist masters, and yogis and yoginis may be helpful in clarifying basic principles—how it all fits together; and why bother in the first place?

Thus it is, mindfulness practice—fully realized or not—transforms the habitually self-referencing "selfing" mind via training in deep, spacious inner peace. The gradual result is a loving, happy, always imperfectly stable mind. Thus does *shamatha* provide support for the vivid clarity and direct wisdom of true *vipashana* realization. While *shamatha* calms the distracted mind, *vipashyana* reveals and stabilizes the nondual view of primordial emptiness, very nature of *dharmakaya*.

Vipashyana

Vipashyana literally means "extraordinary seeing"—penetrating direct clear seeing that is the primordial purity of yogic direct perception (*yogi pratyaksa*)—prior to the reflexive superimposition (*vikshepa*) of discursive conceptual mind. Buddhist *Vipashyana* is "analytic insight meditation".

Such insight is direct, non-conceptual, transpersonal seeing (*samadhi*, Zen *kensho/satori*) of the empty absence of "any shred" of ultimate intrinsic existence of all spacetime phenomena; to wit, the *ultimate* emptiness of all the *relatively* real appearing physical and mental stuff of our busy lifeworld realities. We shall see in these pages that this initially rather offputting radical emptiness notion becomes the main source of our human happiness. And yes, it requires kind patient practice, and a bunch of courage.

So, *vipashyana* insight transcends but embraces clear thinking through clear *direct* seeing. Here the knowing subject does not merely intend its object of knowledge, but is aware of the direct *feeling* experience of being already present in it, with no distance or separation at all. Again, just for a moment, settle now into the breath in the belly and *feel* the bright delight of "primordially pure" seeing without thinking about it!

Hence, *shamatha* and *vipashyana* meditation together liberate perception and conception from their habitual and constricted experience of the myriad objects arising in objective time, with all their random and wandering distractions, thereby permitting the gaze of the mind to settle into, and rest in its subjective, innermost body of present moment, here now bright "feeling experience". This is the bodily location of human happiness. It happens upon the breath. Remain close to the breath.

English poet William Blake called this healing purification of awareness of our constant objective inherently dualistic thinking—"cleansing the doors of perception".

In this way are Aldous Huxley's "doors of perception" opened wide to the "micro-phenomenological" purity of our inter-subjective, direct present moment blissful "feeling experience", prior to the dualistic semiotic conceptual contraction that is our all too human deep cultural background (unconscious) materialist "global web of belief" (Quine 1969).

Thus, upon an encounter with a lovely red rose, we drop our "expectational bias" about its objective meaning—"Yes, that's a red rose"—and encounter it intimately with all of our sensory, aesthetic, and feeling awareness. It is by way of meditation that we "stop to smell the roses" of our feeling nature—our affective, awake and delightful "lived experience". Stop and see for yourself.

This intrapersonal *awareness management skill set* changes everything. It enriches the dance of both verbal and nonverbal interpersonal awareness in our relationships with those within our sphere; and especially with our most beloved. Greatly enhanced human happiness and well being is the wondrous result, as many of you well know.

Thus do our arising realities become the subtle feeling experience of poetry. Thus does the shaman-poet dwelling in mythtime, at the root of attention and just prior to the world, sing,

> Everything is alive!
> Trees, grasses, wind dancing,
> guides me. I understand
> the songs of the birds!

"The poet's eye, in a fine frenzy rolling, doth glance from heaven to earth, from earth to heaven" (Wm. Shakespeare). Thus do we unify the lucent heaven of our divine nature with the fervent earth of our bodily existence.

Wisdom Mind No-Self Help

But wait! If "I change my mind, and so change my brain" (Begley 2007) by meditation, I fear that I might "tune in and drop out" of life, quit my job, leave my family as did the Buddha, join some cult, get on drugs, and wind up on the streets, or worse.

Psychologists have a name for such fearful cognition: "catastrophic expectations". We're all a little frightened of change. Not to worry. As the prodigious self-ego-I becomes *gradually* aligned with your compassionate love-wisdom mind Presence of this vast primordial whole, committed meditation practitioners still show up for work, pay the bills, and change diapers. All the attractive and aversive stuff of always thinking, furiously desirous self-ego-I that we have come to know and love still exists in abundance in our conventional, *relatively*, really real "real world out there" (RWOT). So stuff still exists.

It's just that all this physical and mental stuff of form doesn't exist absolutely or *ultimately*. In the really big picture, as Buddha told, "Form is empty; emptiness is form". So we, as a separate self, need not get hung up on the absolute reality of it. We learn to chill out and stop taking our ego life drama so seriously. We learn to drop our spooky "conformational bias"—that all new data are interpreted as supporting our current skeptical "global web of belief"—and adopt the refreshingly open *shoshin* cognitive posture of our already present peaceful Zen mind/Buddha mind. Perhaps we are not the center of the universe after all. Now that's a scary thought!

Try this. Return for one minute to your love-wisdom mind Presence. Then say to yourself: "Self, as open Buddha Mind Presence, *What* do I feel in this very moment now? If I feel happy, *how* did I do it? If I do not feel happy, *how* did I do that? *Who* is it that acts out this comedy-drama of my life? Who am I , really? *What* is really real, and not so real. *What* is the most important thing for me to feel, and to do right now? *How* will I feel it? How will I do it? *When* is the best time to do it?

Avoid "Why" questions. They have little practical positive value and lead to ego-self-stimulating, often negative speculation and conceptualization. For example, "Why do I continue to do this, and that?" "Why can't I stop thinking/doing this, and that?" "Why is my boss such a jerk?" "Why won't I establish an effective meditation practice?" "Why does the world exist?" "Why does $E = mc^2$?" "Why" questions are usually "How" questions in disguise. "Why" questions are often more productive when converted to "How" questions.

Be that as it may, all of this *relative* form and our thinking about it is absent and empty of any permanent *ultimate* existence. Appearing spacetime reality is not as it appears! Our self-ego-I is not nearly as real as it appears! We change our view and belief about reality a bit—away from self and toward our selfless Buddha mind—and a lot of our anxiety and suffering drops away.

Really understanding this unity of Buddha's Two Truths—relative form its ultimate emptiness—imperfectly frees us from fear and anger, and thus opens our hearts and minds to our always present Presence of *bodhicitta*—benefiting living beings—which is after all, the main secret of human happiness. And this places the unruly narcissistic self in its "supreme identity"—our primordial Buddha love-wisdom mind—bright always present Presence of That. Everyone in our sphere of influence benefits, especially those we love the most.

As Buddha told so long ago, "Wonder of wonders, all beings are Buddha".

So, that is more or less the Buddhist Mahayana view of the Path of meditation. We align a diaphanous empirically unfindable and unprovable yet conventionally all too real unruly self with selfless Buddha mind Presence, more or less moment to moment, and skillfully work and play in a beautiful, relatively real, but not ultimately real world with enhanced peace, and often great happiness.

Contrary to an all too common misunderstanding about Buddhism, we are not required to give up, put down, or otherwise abolish our self-ego-I! Buddha's way is to work with it, lift and align it with our always present Buddha love-wisdom mind, all the while remaining aware of ego's very subtle duplicity. Buddha mind "is already accomplished from the very beginning", deep within us, here and now. It is That to which we awaken—step by mindful step—upon the Buddhist Path.

Therefore, "Leave it alone and let it be as it is". No need to *try* to change anything at all. Rather, simply place your attentional awareness upon your subtle always already present Buddha nature/Buddha mind. Bright Presence of That.

So now, just for this precious moment, experience profound thankfulness for your precious life, just as it is now, imperfections, pain, worry and all. Feel that gratitude within your heart of hearts. Then feel your good will intention to benefit living beings, however imperfectly. No need to fabricate it. It's already present. Open to receive it.

Begin and end each day with this selfless affirmation: "Thank you for the gift of my life, just as it is now". This will help you to stay present to Presence of your Buddha nature/Buddha mind—your already present Heart's desire. *Feel* for a moment this post-conceptual peace of mind. Now know that there is nothing other than this. Practice that—"brief moments, many times"—amid all of the myriad distractions.

Through such wisdom mind considerations we come to see clearly that our habitual thoughts and feelings have no real substance in themselves—but are rather an apparitional will-o'-the-wisp, utterly dependent upon our constantly changing distracted and unfocused mind states. Thus arises all-important loving self-acceptance, like the unfailing love of the mother for her frightened child. From that Great Love spontaneously arises loving-kindness and acceptance of others.

We now begin to see the humor of our absurd, obsessive self-referential story-narrative—why I-Me-Mine is always right, never wrong; and always the center of the universe. If everyone acted like that the world would be in a real mess. The bad news: everyone *does* act like that! And the world *is* in a real mess. We need your help. We're all in this reality boat together.

True, some of the "slings and arrows of outrageous fortune" are abated as our compassionate intrapersonal relationship with our indwelling love-wisdom mind Presence grows, and through that our interpersonal relationships flourish (even with "difficult people").

Still, much of the natural adversity that mortal flesh is heir to remains unabated. We never get enough of the stuff we want; and we get far too much of what we don't want. And we're still impermanent (*anitya*), living in the constant presence of our physical death. And that requires courage; the courage not to fall into readily available ego defenses that sublimate our powerful onto-pathological deep fear of nonexistence into the endless outer distractions of work and play. So, *stop* and smell the roses. Love-wisdom mind Presence, it is said by those who know, has a very subtle aroma of roses.

Awareness Management.

What is it that changes with the Buddha's "mindfulness of breathing"? It is our habitual *reaction* to adversity; and our *response* to that opportunity! Anxiety, anger, and dread lose most of their power over us. That is to say, we no longer *choose* to submit to the negative stuff. We choose instead to place our awareness—amid myriad distractions—upon our quiescent mantra breath, always present mindful Presence of That. That is the simple practice of the Path. What a relief! But just reading about it means very little. Yes, fortunately, mindfulness practice must actually be practiced.

So, with our attention nearly always placed upon the love-wisdom Buddha mind Presence that rides each mindful mantra breath we are, however imperfectly, at peace.

Thus is human happiness very much a matter of awareness management. Human happiness is, very pragmatically, a direct result of where we choose to place our present attentional awareness, moment to moment, here and now. That is our instant connection to innermost peace.

We have more control over our *present* mind state than we may have imagined possible. Our continuity of mindful awareness practice, "brief moments, many times", makes it so.

Abiding calmly in this centrist Buddhist (and centrist Hindu, Taoist, Judaic-Christian) Middle Way view and practice, things aren't nearly so worrisome. Our lived experience is all the more vivid and beautiful. Ultimately, in the proverbial final analysis, even as we live in the uncertainty and impermanence of this "dark cloud of unknowing", "there is no problem whatsoever in this world" (Suzuki Roshi). That is the aboriginal wisdom of all embracing dimension of Ultimate Truth, our selfless Big Mind that pervades and embraces this all too real world of fraught Small Mind conventional Relative Truth.

Just so, these two reality realms are utterly indivisible, an always already prior and present non-conceptual, nondual inseparable unity—bright Presence of That. Such a peace may be beyond discursive, conceptual understanding; but it is readily present to our feeling mind, our contemplative indwelling love-wisdom Buddha mind, when we *remember* to open to receive, and then retain it. So, breathe mindfully right now for a few moments. Rest in that bright "unborn, unceasing, uncreated"," mind space between your thoughts. Well, when is the best time to do it? Yes. Now is the time.

The key principle that grounds contemplative practice is this: both human happiness and human suffering arise from our present mind state! So, we consciously manage our awareness by taming and training the "wild horse of the mind" in placement of attention on our innermost indwelling love-wisdom mind Presence (vidya, rigpa). *In Buddhism this process of the Path begins with calm abiding* (shamatha) *upon the breath, beyond our thoughts and beliefs* about *it.*

Basic Mindfulness Practice: Quieting the Wild Horse of the Mind

The subtlest, nondual "innermost secret" practices of *Dzogchen*, Essence *Mahamudra*, Definitive *Madhyamaka*, *Saijojo* Zen, all begin with mindful *shamatha*. "Secular" mindfulness practice also begins, and often ends here. Fear and bias against human cognitive religious/spiritual depth is taboo in "scientized" Western culture. How is this so?

Due not only to our fear of the deep subjectivity of the unknown, but to the objectivist bias of our deep cultural background Western ideology—Scientific Materialism/Physicalism that has entirely colonized the Western mind—there exists a powerful sociocultural taboo against moving our secular mindfulness meditation practice beyond mere breathing techniques to anything more deeply subjective—like human cognitive state/stage four perfectly subjective nondual yogic experience (*yogi pratyaksa*).

Secular mindfulness, while highly beneficial in managing stress, and some psycho-emotional disorders, limits cognitive experiential depth to state one perceptual, state two conceptual, and early state three contemplative state and life stages (cf. *Introduction* above). For the practitioner to penetrate more deeply into the primordial nature of mind the objective, subjective and spiritual guidance of a meditation master is required. After all, That love-wisdom mind nature is who we actually are—our "supreme identity".

Be That as it may, wouldn't it be nice to *directly* experience that primordial love-wisdom mind Presence that you already are? There's no time like the present.

Therefore, bracket for a moment your present quiescent practice, if you have one, and all your questions and beliefs—just for this precious moment now—and give yourself *two minutes* of peace. It's easier than you think. If you find this following mindfulness practice useful, the Buddha has some surprising suggestions to deepen your practice, and enhance your present happiness. Mindful caveat: You cannot learn, nor experience the basic space of *shamatha* mindfulness by reading about it. It must be assiduously practiced.

"Without past, present, future; empty awake mind" (Ju Mipham Rinpoche).

Your Mindfulness Practice: Ten Steps to Bliss. Sit up straight, uncross your legs, cast your partially closed, unfocused eyes down slightly so that your neck is straight, and place your attention upon the breath in your belly. Relax jaw, neck, gut. Experience the breath naturally rising and falling in the belly. *Feel* that.

1. *Opening Prayers and Refuge.* Thank you! First, briefly experience deep gratitude for the great gift of your life exactly as it is now. Then feel your great good will intention that your life

may benefit living beings. This affirmation is most important. It opens the heart and mind to receive selfless grace by shifting attention from self to the benefit of others.

Refuge Prayer: "Until the full *bodhi* of enlightenment, I take refuge in the Buddha, the dharma, and the *sangha*".

2. *Attention!* Now, with eyes open, gather the "wild horse of the mind" by *placement of attention* upon your breath as it rhythmically, naturally arises in your belly. Breathe normally. Just for this moment—without grasping at, or rejecting anything—witness your awareness. Be reflexively aware of your awareness; of the *prana/spirit* life force current that animates you with each and every breath. Stay and be present only to your breath.

3. *The Polyvagal Breath.* Continue with eyes open. Breathe in normally for five seconds; then out for seven seconds, through pursed lips, like breathing out through a small straw. Practice this for three, seven, or nine times, as you wish. Then breathe normally. Polyvagal breathing interrupts the production of cortisol, the stress hormone, produced by the adrenal cortex. This inhibits its flow along the vagus nerve (CN-X) which innervates all the organs of the parasympathetic nervous system—heart, lungs, digestive—instantly reducing the "fight or flight" stress response (Porges 2014).

Now, with each breath feel your busy mind settle into its natural state of wakefulness—your clear light love-wisdom mind Presence—that aspect of you that is utterly one with the great source of everything—your safe place, free of thoughts, concepts, beliefs; free of past and future; free of judgment, fear, anger, guilt, and pride; momentarily free of narcissistic self-ego-I. No need to think about it, or fabricate it. Open and feel it. Be that stillness now. *Feel* this peace that passes all understanding.

4. *Prana: The Spirit Wind.* Now, with eyes open or closed, feel life force energy of gentle *prana* spirit wind—the very "breath of life"—as it enters in upon the breath, then pervades every

space of your body and mind—all physical, mental, emotional, spiritual structures. *Prana, c'hi, lung, pneuma*-Holy Spirit is the subtle form of gross spacetime physical light energy/matter form ($E = mc^2$) arising continuously from formless, spacious, vast boundless whole, basic space (*dharmadhatu*), formless primordial awareness-consciousness ground itself (*dharmakaya*) in whom you, and all of this spacetime form arises, participates, and is happily instantiated.

Enjoy this feeling of delight within you. Feel your connectedness to everything. No need to try to create it. Your mindful Presence upon the breath is always already present now. That is your "supreme identity". Who am I? That I Am! Feel That. It is That to which you awaken upon the mindful breath.

5. *Your Alpha Breath Posture.* Now, with your gaze still slightly downward, briefly close your eyes, raise your eyebrows and focus attention behind your forehead. Feel a subtle, focused fullness in your forebrain. You are now *directly* experiencing subtle, but observable waking *alpha* and *theta* brain rhythm—the non-conceptual "relaxation response" which replaces "fight or flight" stress response. Breathe and enjoy. Notice here the profound sense of your luminous wisdom mind Presence. Magnify and amplify it. No need to think about it; simply feel its lush emotional texture.

6. *Let Being Be.* Now, slightly open your eyes. As the mind begins to wander from the breath, thoughts and feelings naturally arise. No problem. *Whatever arises, let it be as it is.* No need to grasp at, or reject anything at all. No need to try to "meditate"; or to stop thinking; or to block troublesome thoughts; or to *try* to do anything at all. There is no goal. Just breathe. Always return to the breath in the belly. Simply remain present to your breath—again and again. That is your basic meditation. Simple enough, but not too simple. As Einstein told, "Make everything as simple as possible, but not simpler".

Without your attention, thoughts and feelings "self liberate" at the very instant of their arising. They dissolve and pass on the out breath. Or watch them gently flow by like a cloud in the vast empty sky, leaving no trace. *Choose* to transfer your attention from busy thoughts and feelings to that spacious sky-like source of the mind—again and again. That is the simple process of "mindfulness of breathing."

More or less absent thoughts and concepts, and the emotions they induce, your post-empirical, non-conceptual Buddha mind Presence is revealed just as it is—luminous and clear. Kind compassionate activity of love spontaneously arises from That. As your mind is filled with spacious, unifying clear light wisdom of love, little space remains for the negative stuff.

As Buddha told so long ago, "Let it be as it is and rest your weary mind; all things are perfect, exactly as they are ... .Wonder of wonders, all beings are Buddha".

So, briefly greet whatever arises—positive, negative, neutral—then label it *"distraction"*, and return your *attention* to the breath, again and again. Your happiness and peace ride the mindful breath.

Now say to the busy mind: "Peace, be still". Say to the grasping self, "Peace, I Am". Let it be so.

Presence Now. Now, with eyes partially open, *feel* your present connection to indwelling love-wisdom Presence that you actually are, by whatever name, right here upon each mindful breath. Rest for a couple of minutes, or more, in this spacious primordial essence-nature of mind—your always already present Buddha mind—by whatever concept or belief. Directly experience, and enjoy.

7. *Mantra Practice.* If you wish to add the great Buddhist mantra *OM AH HUM*, or *OM MANI PADME HUM* (*Appendix A*) to your *alpha* breath practice, please do so. It's a touchstone that will aid in managing distractions, and subtly, instantly connect you to the inherent power of your *bodhi* mind Presence. Mindful practice brimming with mantra prayer has little space for distraction! Remain present to mantra— "brief moments, many times"—in your cognitive foreground

or background throughout the day and night. Please give yourself this gift of light, one minute, several times a day, and through the long night.

8. *Real Practice.* A: Practice all steps immediately upon rising for 15-30 minutes, or longer; B: practice your alpha mantra breath only, 15-60 seconds during the day "brief moments many times: C: practice all steps 10-20 minutes just before sleep with emphasis on quiescent peace of mind. These three will establish a profound continuity of enlightened awareness day and night. Evening practice is especially important if you have sleep troubles (*Appendix A*). *Be* the entire night in your love-wisdom mind Presence. Let this be your love-wisdom lullaby and good night.

9. *Dream Work Practice.* Upon arising, before meditation, very briefly write down important dream *images*. A dream narrative is not required. Primary images only. No need to "analyze" the dream; or try to figure out "what it means". "Work the dream" in the first person tense. Speak as the key person, or image in the dream thusly: "*I am*—, and *I feel*—. Don't talk *about* the image. *Be* the image. *Feel* the image as if it were you. It's your dream after all. Do this with a loved one if possible. You will find it most revealing. Now practice your morning meditation as usual; and be present to key dream images.

    Encourage your dream life toward lucid dreaming. Soon, with "good karma" and a bit of luck, you will consciously enter the blissful "Pure Land of Sukavati". Pray for this.

10. *The Dedication of Merit.* Now, close this and all practice sessions, of whatever length, by "dedicating the merit" and goodness generated by your practice to the benefit, happiness, and ultimate liberation of all living beings. Utter this great aspiration: "*By this good may all beings be free of suffering, and the causes of suffering. May all beings have happiness, and the causes of happiness—for as long as space remains*". This bodhisattva *bodhicitta* intention shifts self-centered practice from merely benefiting self—which it certainly does—to the

benefit of both self and all living beings. Astonishingly, this is the very best way to be happy yourself! As if self and no-self were ever separate at all.

The mindful upshot of all this noise about quiescence? Simply rest in your always present Buddha nature of mind. As distractions inevitably arise, return to your mindful mantra breath, again and again. Such patience and diligence will establish a deep, subtle, peaceful and abiding continuity of your innate love-wisdom mind— luminous Presence of That. *Emaho!* How wonderful! *Mahasukaho!* Ultimate Happiness Itself!

If you wish to greatly enhance your practice please open your heart and mind to a qualified meditation mentor/master—a "spiritual friend", and a spiritual community. This shall readily increase your effectiveness in the world, and your happiness with the world.

The Bodhisattva Vow. After a few months, or a few years of practice you may wish to consider this vow. Should you choose to do so, ask your teacher, or better yet your Lama, Roshi, or Ajahn to witness it. Without further comment, here is the Bodhisattva Vow, "Refuge Heart" of the Buddhist Mahayana-Vajrayana teaching vehicle:

Just as all the Buddhas have generated bodhicitta, the mind of enlightenment, and accomplished the stages of the Bodhisattva Path, so will I, for the benefit of living beings, accomplish that same path. Until then, I take refuge in the Buddha, the dharma, and the sangha.

From 8th century Middle Way Madhyamaka *Mahasiddha* Shantideva:

May precious bodhicitta take its birth
In those in whom it has not taken birth.
And where it has been born, let it not cease,
But increase ever more and more.
—*The Bodhisattva's Way of Life*

For the complete *Brief Course*, visit *Appendix A*, "Let It Be: Basic Mindfulness Meditation". Please review these two supports for your practice—the above "Mindful Ten Steps to Bliss", and *Appendix A*—weekly, until it becomes natural. The Bibliography offers a basic reading list for contemplative study.

Review of The View

The analytic "penetrating insight" that is liberating *vipashyana* reveals this great nonlocal (beyond time and space), nondual (subject-object unity) truth of the *buddic* wisdom of emptiness/*shunyata*, that we may utilize it in selfless service of sentient beings—compassionate *bodhicitta*—being here in time and form.

For esoteric Tibetan Vajrayana practice mindful *shamatha*, *vipashyana* and *bodhicitta* are the View and Path that bears the Fruit or Result of realization of the inseparable, indivisible unity of: 1) arising, appearing phenomena and emptiness; 2) of vivid clarity and emptiness; and 3) of bliss and emptiness.

Therefore, *shamatha* mindfulness bestows peace of mind that opens into *vipashyana* (and many other practices)—selfless open awareness Presence (*vidya, rigpa*) that facilitates entering in direct penetrating insight of the very nature of mind—intimate, mostly concept free liberation that is our "supreme identity" with the vast spacious, empty boundless whole (*dharmadhatu*) of appearing reality itself (*dharmakaya*). *Emaho!*

In whom does this all arise? It is this ultimate primordial awareness-consciousness itself, numinous vast whole in whom relative human awareness-consciousness is always a luminous instantiation. We are never separate from That. Good to know as we go through the days, and the nights of our lives. Knowing this changes everything!

However, there is no need to *believe* any of this. The Buddhadharma is less concepts and beliefs, and more direct experience. As Buddha told so long ago,

> O Monks, do not believe what I teach
> out of respect for me. Come and see.

The Neuroscience of Meditation and Our Experience of Self

What are the neurobiological influences of mindfulness meditation on human behavior; how do these influences effect our sense of self-ego-I; our brain structure and function; relative human flourishing; and ultimate happiness and freedom of the liberation from suffering, enlightenment, and Buddhahood?

Buddhist masters and neuroscientists agree, "mindfulness of breathing" ("focused attention meditation"), and "compassion meditation" both facilitate 1) a beneficial shift of attention from obsessive, usually fraught *self-referential thinking* and concern for "I, Me, Mine"; which 2) bestows a sense of inner peace and self-acceptance; which 3) reduces anxiety and anger toward self and others; which 4) enhances altruistic thought, intention and action for the benefit of all living beings, 5) enhancing personal well being and happiness. How shall we understand this cognitive process in the gloss of neurobiology?

Unfocused, ruminating, wandering mind, under sway of the brain's "default mode network"—the medial prefrontal cortex (MPFC) and posterior cingulate cortex (PCC)—significantly increase self-referential attention—"selfing"—with its always present fear/anxiety, anger/hostility, greed/pride, and negative judgments about self, which are then projected onto others. The micro-cognitive result of such negative emotion in the individual is stress, ill-will, and unhappiness. The macro-cognitive result in the collective human sociocultural cognosphere is alienation, despotism, war, and endless suffering.

Scientific meta-research, synthesizing data from thousands of research projects since about 1970, reveal that all three of the classes of meditation—1) mindfulness focused attention (usually upon the breath); 2) open monitoring mindfulness (witnessing whatever arises in awareness without judging, grasping or rejecting); and 3) loving-kindness compassion meditation (feeling our natural empathy for living beings)—conclusively reduced or deactivated processing in some physical brain structures, while enhancing activity in others.

Just so: 1) Meditation reduced processing in the default mode network (PCC and MPFC) of the "selfing" wandering mind; which 2) reduced self-ego-I self-referential processing—habitual attention and concern about I-Me-Mine with its attendant anxiety, anger and ill-will mind states; 3) reduced activity in, and reduced physical size of the amygdala which is responsible for fear and anger ("fight or flight"); 3) reduced stress related cortisol production by the adrenal cortex while blocking cortisol circulation throughout the upper body upon the autonomic vagus nerve (CN-X); 4) enhanced beneficial brain *alpha, theta,* and high amplitude *gamma* band oscillations (25 to 42 hertz), while reducing excessive beta activity; 5) reduced activity in the right prefrontal cortex which is active in fear, anger, and ill-will mind states; 6) greatly increased left prefrontal cortex processing which enhances feelings of altruism, compassion and forgiveness toward self and others; 7) induced increased, long term frontal cortex gyrification (neuroplasticity), which is permanent, even when contemplative practice ceases (Siegel 2013; Porges 2014; Begley 2007; Wallace 2007, 2009; *Scientific American,* November, 2014).

The no longer surprising result of this neuroscientific meta-research is greatly reduced preoccupation with self and its obsessive narcissistic self-narrative; reduced psycho-emotional stress; induced and enhanced subjective feelings of connection, well being, good will, and subjective reports of increased happiness.

Thus does mindfulness and other types of meditation train the "wild horse of the mind" in the *placement of attention,* and continued focus of awareness upon immediate, non-conceptual, present moment to moment sensory/feeling experience, upon the mindful breath—our eternal here and now connection—while shifting attention away from chronic unfocused wandering mind with its obsessive and unhappy attachment to self-ego-I.

Therefore, meditation clearly reduces or suspends the "selfing" that causes the terrible suffering secondary to our pervasive sense of a lonely, separate, fearful mortal self. And all of this through a program of mind training in present moment, trans-conceptual *feeling awareness* upon the breath—the placement and maintenance of attention upon the breath which settles the "wild horse of the mind" upon the very source and "nature of mind", boundless all embracing whole, nondual love-wisdom mind Presence of That, by whatever name or concept.

Yes, neuroscientific research demonstrates the profound value of meditation—especially *shamatha* calm abiding, and loving-kindness compassion meditation—in support of human flourishing and happiness. Indeed, there is a "mindfulness revolution" now abroad in the Western mind and its culture. Mindfulness training is alive and well in most of our institutions: education, medicine, psychology, the social sciences, business, government, military, and corrections.

This Western mindfulness cognitive reconstruction has even entered monotheistic organized religion—Judaism, Christianity, Islam. Abrahamic Monotheism has lost— under sway of the dominant cognitive paradigm that is Greek-animated proto-theistic Scientific Materialism/Physicalism (which has now colonized the Western mind)—much of its foundation in the contemplative mythos and praxis of the highest nondual (subject-object unity) teaching of our great Primordial Wisdom Tradition—Hinduism, Buddhism, Taoism, Judaism, esoteric/mystical Christianity, Islam.

On this neurobiological view, human happiness is very much dependent upon an *awareness management skill set*—where, when, and how we *choose* to place our attentional awareness. In short, both happiness and unhappiness are the result of our *choices* as to present *placement of attention*—negative emotions, or love-wisdom mind Presence—each moment now. Mindful awareness practice makes it so.

Cognitive neuroscience has identified two ways of experiencing the self—two modes of self-reference: 1) *narrative focus upon self*, our urgent all consuming story-drama about ourselves; and 2) *experiential focus*, bodily proprioceptive sense experience, with direct trans-conceptual feeling experience. These two modes are often hypothesized by cognitive scientists to be neurologically distinct. Buddhism has unified them.

Once again, volumes of research have demonstrated that in both meditators and non-meditators alike the *experiential focus* mode involving non-conceptual "mindfulness of breathing" as the Buddha called it, reduced egocentric narrative self-referential activity—in a word "selfing"—in the MPFC and PCC of the default mode network.

However, for highly skilled meditators habitual fantasy-reverie self-referential thinking of the untrained mind is absent during sitting meditation, and for varying periods of time following formal sitting meditation. For these yogis and yoginis processing activity of the default mode network is nearly quiescent (Siegel 2013). These skilled practitioners abide in a "walking meditation" mind state most of the time. And this cognitive state of "calm abiding" persists through several sleep states during the night.

In short, "advanced" meditators have demonstrated in many studies (Begley 2007; Siegel 2013) the capacity to maintain such stable quiescent contemplative mind states, with their corresponding brain rhythms (*theta* and *gamma*) in "post-meditation" activities—while "hewing wood and carrying water", and driving, talking, loving, and even in creative thinking!

Therefore, meditation practice for established meditators seems to facilitate the *choice* of a fluent cognitive ambulation from conceptual self narrative mode to a peaceful, even blissful non-conceptual experiential mode, almost at will. Indeed, the mind states of the nondual mode are usually experienced as pervading and embracing conceptual self narrative mind states. There seems to be no appreciable difference.

The global result of meditation practice in the meditator is calm, abiding, quiescent peace of mind, and a happy felt sense of connection and interdependence with all living things; and indeed, with the unbroken whole of *Kosmos* itself—even as inexorable human adversity continues to arise.

Mindful Thinking About Science and Spirit

We've just seen that hundreds of scientific studies with highly advanced Buddhist meditators, as well as beginning meditators, have demonstrated that subjective meditation states have objective neural correlates in the brain. Well and good. Does this factoid mean that trans-physical, post-empirical meditation experience can be reduced to merely physical brain states, as acolytes of our modern prevailing materialist metaphysic—the "scientific reductionism" of fundamentalist "Scientism"—believe?

Does the fact that Buddhist modernists, for example H.H. Dalai Lama, correctly state that Buddhism is, and has always been a contemplative "science of mind" mean that the Buddhist understanding of mind with its nondual Buddha nature of mind (*buddhadhatu, buddhajnana*) is also an objective science of mind in the same way that experimental psychology, or physics is?

It does not. Is the "mind of enlightenment" taught by all of the buddhas reducible to the mere EEG brightening of the left prefrontal cortex during an advanced meditator's heartfelt compassion for a living being in terrible pain? It is not. Yet, in the highest all-embracing nondual view, it is! It depends upon the view, relative or ultimate.

It is useful here to remember that the spectrum of human knowledge—from the objective conceptual understanding of mathematical physics, to the deep subjectivity of Buddha mind—is, when engaged by discursive concept mind—pervaded by metaphysical, or ontological speculation. And that is pervaded by nondual Buddha mind which embraces all human cognition, dualistic and nondual alike.

Philosophers of science and Buddhist lamas agree: that appearing spacetime reality is *ultimately* objective and material/physical is an unproven, unprovable metaphysical assumption/belief. (*Appendix D*). That reality is ultimately subjective and illusory is equally so. That reality is a centrist middle way between these two metaphysical extremes is still provisional, uncertain, fallible concept and belief. No problem at all. And the trans-conceptual definitive contemplative certainty of nondual Buddha mind? Clearly, that is beyond belief. We are thus naturally referred to deeper, post-empirical contemplative strata of cognitive formation.

Metaphysical scientific reductionism—the epistemological reduction of all appearing reality to mere physical phenomena—is the dogmatic hand maid to our prevailing Western cultural "global web of belief", namely, the much valorized and idealized metaphysic of Scientific Materialism/Physicalism—"Scientism" in its extreme proto-religious fundamentalist cloak.

The "scientific method"—systematic objective observation, measurement, experiment, and the experimental formulation and testing of hypotheses—is wondrously capable of revealing informational truths in the conceptual dimension of objective, physical spacetime appearing reality; the world of physics, cosmology, mathematics, and biology. Yet, such a monistic metaphysic methodologically ignores the entire dimension of subjective, non-conceptual, non-physical human experience, to wit: 1) the bliss of feeling emotional experience of personal and spiritual love; 2) the trans-conceptual contemplative experience of the perfectly subjective nondual primordial love-wisdom of the Buddha and of the Christ; and 3) the great nondual Primordial Wisdom Tradition of humankind that transcends yet embraces and includes the purely objective realm of modern science.

Physical science and our emerging inchoate Western Science of Consciousness, of which East/West contemplative science is a branch, must work together to pragmatically unify our objective conceptual, and subjective contemplative knowledge that is so profoundly displayed through these two complementary sciences, physical/conceptual and contemplative/spiritual. That is our joyous urgent wisdom project as we enter in the 21st century Noetic Revolution that is now upon us. (Boaz 2021b, excerpted at davidpaulboaz.org)

Therefore, nondual primordial awareness wisdom (*jnana, yeshe*), that is expressed through human skillful discriminating wisdom (*prajna, sherab*) which includes objective, empirical, conceptual knowledge, and intuitive mythopoetic knowledge requires that we human beings utilize our innate *noetic cognitive doublet* that constitutes both the objective and subjective voices of the nonlocal, nondual whole of our human love-wisdom mind.

We must understand that these two are an ontologically prior, yet an epistemologically and phenomenally present complementary, indivisible unity. We utilize this handy cognitive doublet to ascertain both provisional and definitive truth, both relative and ultimate truth, and the ontic prior but always present indivisible unity of these two human cognitive modalities. As Guru Rinpoche Padmasambhava told: "We accomplish ultimate truth only through relative truth. Practice these two as a unity". We must keep a holistic view.

Philosophy—*philo-sophia*—Western or Eastern is so much more than sterile academic philosophy. Traditionally, philosophy is the love of wisdom. Ultimately, philosophy is the prior and present unity of love and wisdom. For the spiritual practitioner philosophy is understanding the practical, skillful expression in compassionate conduct of this love-wisdom unity for the benefit of living beings. That is how we may *be* happy now. And that is the Buddha's teaching for the ages.

Kuhnian (Thomas Kuhn's 1961 breakthrough *Structure of Scientific Revolutions*) scientific "paradigm shifts" produce "scientific revolutions" every generation or two. Cases in point: in the 17th century Newtonian Revolution Isaac Newton utilized, but enhanced Galileo's theory of relativity; Einstein's Special Relativity Theory (SRT) enhanced Newton's relativity, and established the present relativistic scientific paradigm. Quantum electrodynamics (QED) corrected and included Einstein's Special and General Relativity Theory (GRT) establishing the present physics Standard Model (lambda cold dark matter/ΛCDM) of particles and fields revealing in the process its own quantum incompleteness, as Einstein was quick to point out.

We are now perched rather precariously upon the cusp of a new knowledge/wisdom paradigm, a Noetic Revolution in matter, mind and spirit (Boaz 2021b) that begins to heal the relentless subject-object split between our objective and subjective cognitive modes of experience. Buddhist contemplative studies is facilitating this process as dialog continues between physicists, philosophers of physics, and practicing Buddhist scholars. And we need a lot more of it.

Therefore, lest we valorize too much in our clinging to the descending "scientific" metaphysic that is modern Scientific Materialism/Physicalism let us understand that all dualistic scientific and Buddhist theories are fallible, provisional and incomplete; impatiently awaiting that next more inclusive, syncretic but ever incomplete theory.

Just so, dualistic Buddhist dialectics—the two thousand year old colloquy that produced the Four Buddhist Tenet Systems—remains incomplete. We shall soon see that it is completed in the ultimate truth union of Buddhist *Dzogchen* and *Mahamudra*. Incompleteness is the destiny of conceptual, dialectical, relative conventional truth, whether scientific or religious. Absolute *objective* certainty remains a pipe dream.

Clearly, the neuroscientific implications of meditation for the reduction of human suffering, and for human happiness are profound. Mindfulness meditation and loving-kindness meditation offer skillful regulation of negative emotional response to life's inexorable adversity by transforming the painful narcissistic self-narrative into peaceable, and altruistic states of mind.

We have now seen that through the assiduous practice of the Buddhist Path we learn to place our present moment to moment awareness—our *attention*—upon our trans-conceptual direct yogic (*yogi pratyaksa*) *feeling experience* of our innate already present Buddha nature/ Buddha mind. *This contemplative process opens a finite awareness portal into infinity wherein we connect with an aspect of ourselves that is selfless, non-conceptual, and profound.* We come to understand that we need not believe and defend our adventitious dreary and destructive negative ego-centric thoughts and feelings; stress is reduced; and human happiness is enhanced.

The psychological/emotional takeaway is this: our all too human mind—thoughts and feelings, positive and negative—are fleeting, inherently evanescent, ever changing, empty (*shunyata*), and impermanent (*anitya*). Knowing this, we, as self-ego-I, give them as much power as we choose. We do have this choice. Contemplative practice makes it so. Perhaps we might take ourselves less seriously, and with a bit of ego-self-effacing humor.

Thus does the Buddha's Fourth Noble Truth of the Path, with the Six Perfections, and the altruistic ethic of *bodhicitta*, result in ultimate happiness of liberation from ignorance (*avidya, marigpa*) that is the root cause of human suffering. The Buddhist Path provides a practical, contemplative way to remain present, moment to moment, to our already present, innermost Buddha mind—happy bright Presence of That. That is the Buddha's promise of primordial awakening to all of us—without a single exception.

Buddhist Dzogchen: Being Happiness Itself

Without past, present, future, empty awake mind.

— Ju Mipham Rinpoche

Fundamental Innate Mind of Clear Light

That is the inherent love-wisdom mind basis of *Dzogchen* View and Practice. *Dzogchen* is the "clear light absolute space of all phenomena". *Dzogchen*, the Great Perfection is considered, by those who know, to be a radically simple, but very difficult path to realization of our all-pervading nondual primordial wisdom (*jnana, yeshe*) ground (*dharmakaya, gzhi rigpa*). How is this so?

Dzogchen Ati Yoga works directly—prior to conceptual Mahayana Buddhist dialectics, and to esoteric Vajrayana tantric mantra and deity practice—with our already present indwelling Buddha nature/Buddha mind (*buddhadhatu, buddhajnana*), the very nature of mind, luminous clear light wisdom Presence of *rigpa* itself, before any arising of phenomenal appearances through their all-embracing boundless spacelike emptiness/*shunyata dharmakaya* ground.

> The original mode of being of all phenomena is innate primordial wisdom. It pervades all grounds (and paths). It is the pristine nature that is present in the mind-streams of all of us beings, from aphids up to buddhas, with no distinction as to good or bad, big or small ... The mind of the Buddha is realized and actualized by nondual *arya* individuals ... The essence of the sugatas pervades all beings (who are) endowed with the essence of the tathagatas (Buddhas) ...

Perfect awakening is attained in the culmination of non-meditation (the fourth yoga of Mahamudra). In that regard, by accomplishing the supreme union of quiescence (*shamatha*) and insight (*vipashyana*) … the taste of absolute space and primordial wisdom, the fruition of the *dharmakaya* and the two *rupakayas* is actualized (*The Great Instructions*).
—Karma Chagmé, *Naked Awareness* (trans. B. Alan Wallace)

It is that primordial awareness essential wisdom nature of mind—the nondual ("not one, not two" subject-object unity) state of undistracted and unfabricated "non-meditation" Presence that is at first "introduced" directly, non-conceptually, to the prepared aspirant by the *Dzogchen* master. It is that luminous awareness in which we learn to tame and settle the "wild horse of the mind", then rest in the very Buddha nature of mind itself. It is That in which we train the unruly self-ego-I of the human mind.

Nondual *Dzogchen* has arisen in the context of the "old translation" ancient Nyingma school (8th century) of the Mahayana Middle Way Madhyamaka Buddhist teaching. Nondual *Essence Mahamudra* has arisen from the "new translation" Kagyu school. Both represent the subtlest or "highest" teaching of Gautama Shakyamuni the Buddha. The union of *Dzogchen* and *Mahamudra* is the realization of the unity of samsara and nirvana. Tsele Natsok Rangdröl:

Mahamudra and Dzogchen differ in words, but not in meaning. The only difference is that Mahamudra stresses mindfulness while Dzogchen rests within awareness itself.

In the clear words of recent Nyingma *Dzogchen* master Tulku Urgyen Rinpoche:

In short, in Mahamudra you train with outer appearances, and in Dzogchen you train with inner rigpa … All appearances are beyond benefit and harm. In this way rigpa and appearances are a unity … The word unity has great significance. Don't divide appearances as being there and awareness as being here. Let appearance and awareness be indivisible...

If you recognize the essence, then when forms appear, they become the unity of appearance and emptiness... Appearing and being empty occur as a unity... The Dzogchen teachings refer to this as the unity of primordial purity (*kadag*) and spontaneous presence (*lhundrub*). Since primordial time (these two) have been inseparably united. Through Trekchö you recognize that your own essence is primordial purity. Through Tögal you realize that the nature is spontaneous presence. Neither of these has any self-nature.

What is mind? Guru Rinpoche explains what is called the 'unity of emptiness and cognizance suffused with awareness'... Its essence is empty; its nature is cognizant. Its capacity is that these two cannot be taken apart. That is the meaning of unity, impossible to separate.

(*Vajra Heart Revisited*, 2020, Rangung Yeshe)

Hence, in *Dzogchen* View and Practice the primordial awareness state of Presence (*rigpa, vidya*) is not dependent upon, nor distracted by external or internal appearances arising in mind. Whatever arises, the practitioner rests firmly in the state of nondual awareness, without grasping or rejecting anything at all. But, without the direct recognition (*yogi pratyaksa*) of primordial awareness, how could one train in it? Thus the necessity of dharma study, and a qualified *Dzogchen* master to initiate and guide the practice of the prepared yogi/yogini aspirant.

Wonder of wonders, that *buddic* Presence is alive and awake in the mundane everyday chaos of our "ordinary mind". So, we need not seek it elsewhere, for example in the causes and conditions of buddhahood. From Garab Dorje's *Three Vajra Verses*, "Introduce the state of presence directly.... Remain there without seeking anything at all. That is the meditation". This cannot be told in words, nor in books.

Therefore, nondual Dzogchen View takes the Result/Fruit of buddhahood as the Path itself. The dualistic "lower" Buddhist teaching vehicles take not the result but the *causes* of Buddhahood—dualistic practice—as the Path. For recent *Dzogchen* Master Chögyal Namkhai Norbu:

> Indian Mahayana Sutra and Tibetan Vajrayana Tantra teachings are characterized by the Path of Renunciation and the Path of Transformation, respectively. The method of the nondual *Dzogchen* teaching is the Path of Self-Liberation.

The Path of Renunciation renounces the ignorance (*avidya*) and cognitive obscurations that are the cause of the negative afflictive emotions that cause human suffering. We practice a cause (dharma practice) to gain a desired result (liberation from suffering).

The Path of Transformation is also a dualistic path wherein the practitioner proceeds from non-virtuous "impure vision" to virtue and "pure vision".

However, in the *Dzogchen* Path of Self-Liberation, there is no *concept* of impure and pure vision. In *Dzogchen* vision there is only the always present unity of the nondual state of self-liberation. It is from the inherent freedom of that view that we proceed upon the Buddhist Path. It is from the *bodhicitta* that spontaneously arises from that view that determines the compassionate conduct of this profound Path.

The Buddha told that the result of such selfless altruistic motivation to act is the main cause of human happiness; and the result of self-centered negatively motivated action is the main cause of human suffering. Cultivation of compassionate *bodhicitta* is the only way to authentic *relative* human happiness, and to awake *ultimate* happiness that is liberation from human suffering—Happiness Itself. Without an authentic individual and sociocultural ethic of compassion it is not possible even to begin to address to prodigious problems of human beings in this all too real relative world of pain and suffering.

The root cause of full bodhi mind awaking in all three Buddhist vehicles is the union of wisdom and compassion—these two limbs of the teaching of the Buddha. That the primordial wisdom of emptiness may result in buddha-hood is due to mahakaruna—the great compassion. Just so, mahakaruna may result in buddhahood due to the wisdom that realizes mahashunyata, the great emptiness. Thus did the Buddha teach that in order to be happy being here as honored guests of this phenomenal world of time and space, we must cultivate compassionate relative *"skillful means", but also the* ultimate *primordial wisdom of emptiness—as a nondual unity! In That we take refuge.*

As Guru Rinpoche, Padmasambhava told so long ago:

You accomplish realization of ultimate truth only through the practice of relative truth … Keep your view as high as the sky; and your deeds as fine as barely flour … Descend with the (ultimate) view while ascending with the (relative) conduct. It is most essential to practice these two as a unity.

These two voices of the Buddha's teaching—skillful compassion and the wisdom of emptiness—strike a balance between construing emptiness as nihilistic nonexistence, wherein virtue doesn't much matter; or as eternalist material existence. The view of real, compassionate relative existence, and the absence or emptiness of intrinsic ultimate existence avoids these two metaphysical extremes that are the false dichotomy of *either* existence *or* nonexistence. That is the Buddha's Madhyamaka Middle Way teaching.

Indeed, it is the ultimate emptiness of appearing phenomena that allows their relative interaction in the function of moral conduct. If our phenomenal realities were not ultimately empty of permanent existence, relative change or motion would not be possible. Our "freedom of the will" would be truly illusory. People, stars, galaxies would freeze in their present spacetime locations. In that case how could we change anything at all in this relative world of time and space through our *choice* to practice the Path and engage *bodhicitta* conduct? The Buddha's Path would be but a cynical exercise in futility.

Middle Way Madhyamaka Prasangika realizes this ultimate emptiness of appearing objective reality, and of a self-ego-I that so often apprehends it in ignorance (*avidya, marigpa*) of the truth of the matter. "In terms of that emptiness, there is no distinction between this Madhyamaka view and the *Dzogchen* view" (Lama Gen Lamrimpa 1999).

As to relative conventional objective existence, Longchenpa told, "When you examine closely, there is nothing there to recognize." Nonetheless, the conceptually and verbally imputed objects of our "real world out there" (RWOT), and this ego-I that truly believes in its ultimate existence, still show up for dinner. Fortunately, for both Prasangika and for *Dzogchen* view and practice, this cause and effect reality is still, indeed all too relatively real. So, we still have to show up for work, and arouse and engage our precious *bodhicitta* to benefit living beings. Thus, the Madhyamaka and *Dzogchen* View negate the inherent ultimate existence of the phenomenal world, while affirming its relative-conventional causal/cause and effect existence. Indeed a Middle Way. Nice *concepts*. But what makes it so?

Nondual Non-Meditation on Clear Light Emptiness

It is in nondual *Dzogchen* "non-meditation"—beyond even the quasi-conceptual quiescence of the early stages of *shamatha* meditation—that one may realize ultimate wisdom of the *shunyata*/emptiness of phenomena, the very Buddha nature of mind.

Thus does the ostensible duality of relative mind (*sems*), and the nondual primordial base or ground, primordial awareness itself that is the very nature of mind (*gzhi rigpa*), together rest in the nondual unity of sameness (*samatajnana*). Nagarjuna told it well, "There is not the slightest difference between samsara and nirvana"; between relative truth and ultimate truth. The Buddha's

Two Truths, relative and ultimate, are already an ontic prior, and epistemic present unity—beyond even the slightest separation of knowing subject, and its known objects.

The Nyingma school's Dodrubchen Rinpoche teaches that as primordial awareness arises, the yogi/yogini does not at all feel this absence of the primal subject-object split. Still, the all-consuming flame of the wisdom of emptiness is vividly present to contemplative experience. And that utterly trans-conceptual non-goal directed "non-meditation" is the main difference between nondual *Dzogchen*, and the still conceptual dialectical Madhyamaka Prasangika approaches. While the view of Buddha's *shunyata*, his Two Truths—relative compassion and ultimate wisdom—and the fruition of the Path that is buddhahood itself are the same in Madhyamaka and *Dzogchen*, there is an important difference in the praxis of these two paths:

> Dzogchen practice, which is unmoved by conceptualization, is far more potent for dispelling the obscurations of the mind, and in that sense is regarded as far more profound (than Madhyamaka).
>
> —Gen Lamrimpa Rinpoche 1999

In *Dzogchen,* nondual, non-goal oriented direct "non-meditation" (*yogi pratyaksa*) the diaphanous objects of apparitional phenomenal appearance utterly vanish into their luminous empty aboriginal "groundless ground" as nondual empty *mahashunyata* arises. In the Mahayana Causal Vehicle, and in the "lower" eight vehicles of Nyingma school Vajrayana, contemplative focus remains more or less on quasi-conceptual mindfulness, mantra, and deity practice. Not so in the fruitional Nyingma nondual ninth vehicle—the *Ati Yoga* of *Dzogchen*—where the prepared yogi/yogini simply rests in the *Perfect Sphere of Dzogchen*, primordial *dharmakaya* ground, wholly free of dualistic conceptual cognition.

We shall see below in our "Approaching *Dzogchen* Practice" that nondual *Dzogchen* non-meditation requires both a deep conceptual, and non-conceptual understanding of the primordial wisdom of emptiness, introduced and transmitted under the enlightened guidance of the *Dzogchen* master. Such preparation is required before fruitional *Dzogchen* practice can really begin.

What remains for the meditator of this the radical dissolution of form in the formless emptiness/*shunyata epoché* after we surrender our habitual discursive concept mind and rest in the actual non-dual nature of mind? Non-conceptual lucent already present *buddic* Presence—*rigpa, vidya*—of this "supreme source" remains always at the spiritual Heart (*hridyam*) of the yogi/yogini. Even when we forget. It's always present! The direct experience of our Buddha mind (*buddhajnana*) Presence makes it so.

It is said by those who know that this innate, empty, radiant clear light love-wisdom mind arises, non-conceptually, for all human beings at the moment of death, in deep dreamless sleep, in moments where waking consciousness is unwittingly suspended, in the deep meditation of highly accomplished masters, and in the conscious awareness mindstream of a Buddha.

Told the Buddha, "Form is empty; emptiness is form". Relative form—the five aggregates or *skandhas*—and their selfless ultimate emptiness are an indivisible nondual (subject-object identity) unity. These are Buddha's Two Truths. Everything that arises and appears to sentient awareness is included herein.

It is through a profound understanding of the Two Truths that we perfect the two main facets of the Buddha's love-wisdom Path—compassionate skillful means/method (*upaya*), and the non-dual primordial wisdom of emptiness (*jnana, yeshe*). This then is the conceptual foundation of Middle Way Madhyamaka that opens into the prodigious *Dzogchen* View. No dilemma. No problem at all.

How then shall we understand this interdependence of wisdom and compassion that pervades the View, Meditation, and Conduct of the *nondual Dzogchen* Path?

For all three extant Buddhist vehicles—Hinayana-Theravada, Mahayana, esoteric Vajrayana/Secret Mantra—spacetime stuff and the self that perceives it is empty. Empty of what? For Madhyamaka

Middle Way Buddhists (the fourth and usually considered "highest" of the Four Buddhist Tenet systems)—both Madhyamaka Prasangika and Madhyamaka Yogachara—arising and appearing form is not empty of *existence*. Madhyamaka is not a nihilist view!

Clearly, something exists! Heavy indeed is the yoke of the burden of rejoinder for those nihilist absolute metaphysical idealists—East or West—who would altogether deny this dynamic world of conventionally existing and experienced objective stuff, our "real world out there" (RWOT) that we have come to know and love. It is this all too real self-ego-I after all, who *chooses* to enter the Buddhist Path, and to act in this world of conditioned cause-effect existence for the benefit of living beings. Appearing reality obviously exists. Yet, it does not exist as it appears. How does it exist? Spacetime stuff is relative-conventionally existent, but ultimately non-existent appearing phenomenal form.

For the Tibetan Buddhist Vajrayana tantric tradition, with its highest nondual *Dzogchen*, the Nyingma School Great Perfection or Great Completion is the subtle nondual pinnacle of Shakyamuni the Buddha's teaching. The four schools of the Buddhist Vajrayana teaching vehicle—Nyingma, Gelug, Kagyu, Sakya—all agree.

Tibetan Buddhist Middle Way Prasangika of the Madhyamaka Buddhist tenet system is the doctrinaire foundation upon which the *Dzogchen* view is established. The Madhyamaka Yogachara *Shentong* direct intuition of Buddha nature found in the Yogachara *chittamatra* tradition are equally important *Dzogchen* sources (Pettit 1999).

Middle Way Madhyamaka—with its two sub-schools that are Prasangika and Yogachara—are then the metaphysical, philosophical sources of highest *Ati Yoga* of the Great Perfection. However, *Dzogchen* ethics, and foundational practice preliminaries (*ngöndro*) are found in the yogic practices of the eight "lower" Mahayana and Vajrayana Buddhist teaching vehicles.

Dzogchen View, Path/Meditation, and Result/Fruition presuppose the Ultimate Truth of Buddha nature (*tathagatagarbha*), our ultimate wisdom mind (*jnana, yeshe*) of the emptiness base (*gzhi rigpa*) whose essence is empty, whose nature is clear light luminosity, and whose expression is spontaneous compassionate *bodhicitta*—the thought, intention, and action for the benefit of living beings. More on this tripartite constitution of the Buddha nature of mind below.

Wisdom and Compassion. These are the two limbs of Buddha's teaching; the very bedrock of the whole of the buddhadharma. If a thought or action is wise but not kind, it's not wisdom. If a thought or action is kind but not wise, it's not wisdom.

Tibetan Buddhist Nyingma school views the Buddha's three teaching vehicles or *yanas* of the buddhadharma—Hinayana, Mahayana, and Vajrayana—as the nine vehicles. The first eight are the Mahayana causal vehicles and are based upon the duality of cause and effect—practice this cause now and reap that happy effect later—and so are inherently incapable of liberating the yogic aspirant from the primal atavistic subject-object split. This primal separation is the prodigious false bifurcation of knowing subject and its objects known. This duality between self and other is the root cause of human ignorance (*avidya, marigpa*) with all its attendant suffering. Thus do we require a nondual teaching.

The view and practice of the Great Perfection are grounded in the Vajrayana/Tantrayana subtle esoteric ninth non-causal vehicle—the *Ati Yoga* of *Dzogchen* which is the nondual state of *direct intuition* (*yogi pratyaksa*) of always already spontaneously present (*lhundrub*) Presence (*vidya, rigpa*) of our indwelling primordial Buddha wisdom mind nature (*jnana, yeshe, gnosis*).

The Buddha's Two Truths in *Dzogchen* View and Practice

The dualistic dimension of everyday spacetime Relative Truth (*samvriti satya*, Tib. *kunzog denpa*)—already embraced and subsumed in the boundless whole that is Ultimate Truth (*paramartha satya*, Tib. *don dampa*), *Perfect Sphere of Dzogchen*—is personified as, and grounded in primordial *Adi Buddha* Samantabhadra (*Tib. Kuntazangpo*), the formless *dharmakaya* Buddha in whom form (*rupakaya* as *sambhogakaya* and *nirmanakaya*) arises and is instantiated. These three dimensions constitute the Tibetan Buddhist

Trikaya of the Base or ground (*gzhi rigpa*)—the three buddha bodies (*kayas*) of ultimate reality itself.

This formless, timeless primeval aboriginal dimension that is Ultimate Truth is empty and absent "any shred" of *svabhava* (*rang zhin*)—relative, conceptually imputed, permanent, independent, intrinsic, ultimate/absolute self-existence. Ultimate Buddha mind (*buddhajnana, dgongs pa*) dimension is the perfectly subjective selfless formless primordial "groundless ground" and great potential of relative *svabhava*—omnipresent, appearing spacetime phenomenal form.

Thus it is, conditional form is relatively real, just not intrinsically, ultimately real. Stuff continuously, interdependently arising from the primordial base/ground does not exist as it appears! The stuff of our appearing realities exists only relatively, conventionally, not absolutely or ultimately. Yet here it is, all too real and full of itself throughout relative objective spacetime existence. This view is the wondrous Buddhist Mahayana/Vajrayana dominant Two Truths trope of *Dzogchen* View and Practice.

In the *Great Perfection Aspiration Prayer of Samantabhadra*—primordial *Adi Buddha* of the Ultimate Truth *dharmakaya* dimension—this primordial ultimate ground is revealed thusly (I have taken the liberty of making slight changes to Richard Barron's excellent translation):

Ho! The entire universe of appearance and possibility, of samsara and nirvana, is one ground, two paths, two results. This is the magical display of innate intrinsic awareness, and its recognition or non-recognition.

Due to the aspiration of the all noble Samantabhadra, may all beings awaken to perfectly manifest buddhahood within the palace of the basic space of phenomena!

The primordial ground of all experience is un-compounded. This reflexive self-arising vast expanse of being is ineffable. There are no correct descriptions for either samsara or nirvana. If there is intrinsic awareness of this point, there is buddhahood. If there is no recognition of intrinsic awareness of the ground sentient beings wander in the suffering of cyclic existence.

Therefore, may all sentient beings of the three realms be aware of the ultimate profundity of the ineffable ground of being!

The "one ground" is, as Lama Tsultrim Allione has shown us,

The base or the womb of the great mother ... It is pure latency, depth, radiance, an expanse of emptiness and infinite potency from which the whole universe comes, yet the ground itself is without external radiance or projective (energy/motion) aspects".

The "two paths" arise from the aboriginal, timeless, formless one ground. One of these paths is the pristine *nirvanic* "recognition of intrinsic awareness of the ground" as primordial *Presence* of one's innate, intrinsic dynamic Buddha mind, the very nature of mind that abides in an already prior and always present unity with that primordial ground—utterly inseparable from the ground itself. The *Result* or *Fruition* of this path? "There is buddhahood", already present from the very beginning.

The other path is the path we all have taken—all of us pre-enlightened beings cycling here in samsaric existence—the not so happy *Result* of "non-recognition" (*ignorance, avidya, marigpa* of self-ego-I) of the empty primordial "groundless ground" that is Samantabhadra, our already present Buddha nature (*tatha-gatagarbha*), Buddha mind (*buddhajnana*). The usual result of this path is endless cyclic suffering of birth, old age, sickness, and death. Not a pretty picture. What then shall we do?

It is this second path that provides the opportunity to *choose* to enter in the practice of Buddha's Eightfold Path (*Pali Canon*), and the Six Paramitas of the Mahayana. Through the profound teaching of these vehicles we recognize, then realize the indwelling, "innate intrinsic awareness" of our Buddha mind that was, and is, as *Dzogchen* founder Garab Dorje told so long ago, "already present from the very beginning". It is that primordial love-wisdom mind Presence to which we awaken—step by mindful step—through the Buddhist *Dzogchen* view and practice.

Emptiness of Mind; Emptiness of Self

Twentieth century *Dzogchen* master Tulku Urgyen Rinpoche points out that selfless Buddhist emptiness/*shunyata*—essential nature of primordial *dharmakaya* ground—is not a nihilistic, blank void of nothingness, but as "empty luminous cognizance". *"Emptiness is not empty of the kayas (buddha reality bodies) and of primordial wisdom"*.

Rather, *shunyata* is the empty absolute space (*dharmadhatu*) of *dharmakaya*, radiant clear light primordial awareness base (*gzhi*), formless ultimate nature of form, selfless, innate clear light Buddha nature of mind. Always present bright Presence of That. We experience That non-conceptually, via direct yogic perception (*yogi pratyaksa*). How then shall we conceptually understand this?

We are told by the wise that as one *chooses* to settle the obsessively busy "wild horse of the mind" into, and then rest in *self-less* "open presence" (*rigpa*) of this "natural state of pristine awareness"—Buddha nature/Buddha mind—one realizes that the mind has no past origin, no present location, and no future destiny. The three times—past, present, future—are absent and empty of mind.

The human mind has no physical structure, nor mental form. It cannot be located in the brain, nor is it elsewhere. If the mind were as big as a house, we might thoroughly search the house, but we will not find the mind. Mind therefore, is a present *luminous cognizant emptiness* that is inherently ineffable and ungraspable by any conceptual construct or cognitive modality—relative-conventional or ultimate. Yet, here it is, brimming with the relative conventional realities of space and time.

Just so, self-ego-I that is so relentlessly embedded in this diaphanous apparition of mind, with all the virtuosity of its conceptual affordances, is also empty of intrinsic ultimate existence. It too is empty of past origin, present location and future destiny. This bizarre phantom self entity does not exist in physical body, nor in mental mind, nor elsewhere. Exhausting analytical *vipashyana* examination reveals no *essential* self at all. Thus is self-ego-I confirmed to be wholly empty of any whit of inherent, intrinsic existence. This is the *anatman* or no-self teaching of the Buddha.

Yet, upon the arising of a strong desire (attraction), or a perceived threat (aversion), self arises like a seductive demon, or else a screaming banshee. How then shall we definitively know and feel, directly—beyond analysis—this great truth of the selfless intrinsic luminous boundless emptiness of form that we actually are?

Approaching *Dzogchen* Practice

We tame, then train this obsessively "selfing" conceptual "wild horse of the mind" through quiescent *shamatha* meditation practice (*smriti, sati*) as taught in Sutrayana. This, with the foundational *ngöndro* practices of Tibetan Vajrayana, is the *Dzogchen* approach. In the Great Perfection the nondual indivisibility of the *Dzogchen* View and contemplative *Ati Yoga* non-meditation practice—with selfless compassion for all other beings—is axiomatic.

In beginning practice it is urgent to recognize that a naive duality between a goal-directed "gradual path", and a direct, immediate "nondual" ("not one, not two") *Dzogchen* path is, as is the conceptually contrived distinction between the Buddha's Two Truths—Ultimate and Relative—a false dichotomy that introduces a confounding duality into the *Dzogchen* View and Meditation. The Two Truths of the great Mahayana teaching vehicle are already a prior and always present unity. We must know this. How then shall we enhance our view that we may feel and know the nondual truth of the matter?

We have seen that the dualistic objective dimension of relative-conventional, causal, physical, perceptual and conceptual truth (*samvriti satya*) is already embraced and subsumed in the nondual perfectly subjective dimension of Ultimate Truth (*paramartha satya*). Thus exists the prior ontological and always present epistemological and phenomenological unity of the Buddha's Two Truths. This all-pervading unity is directly experienced (*yogi pratyaksa*) non-conceptually, as feeling knowing certainty of our indwelling Buddha nature/Buddha mind—clear bright light Presence of That—well beyond our conceptual "global web of belief" (Quine 1969) *about* it. Instant, open, knowing-feeling, *maha-ati* "pure Presence" (*vidya, rigpa*) *of* it, by whatever name, is recognition, and in due course, realization of That!

What then shall we do when we inevitably become distracted and forgetful of this great truth of our here now Presence of the nature of mind. The *Dzogchen semdzins*—Vajrasattva mantra (short and long versions), the essential mantra *OM AH HUM*, and the forcefully expressed seed syllable ***PHAT***—are our instant antidote, our *Ati Yoga* awareness touchstones. It is through the non-conceptual *semdzin* that we return our attention to "innermost secret" Presence of the formless ground, the *Perfect Sphere of Dzogchen*, again and again.

False dichotomy caveat: our self-ego-I concept-mind—under sway of ignorance (*avidya, marigpa*)—firmly believes and defends the linguistic semiotic split between dualistic and nondual Path; between Ultimate Truth and Relative Truth; between form and emptiness; between knowing subject and its objects known; between the two illusory *mayas* that are ultimate nondual selfless primordial awareness *Dzogchen vidya maya*, and relative conceptually contrived *avidya maya*; between existence and nonexistence; primordial purity and impurity; nirvana and samsara; dualistic and nondual view and meditation. All of these ultimately indivisible, yet complementary cognitive unities are cloaked in the false dichotomy of dualistic Relative Truth (*samvriti satya, kunzog denpa*) with its cognitive reticulum of "concealer" concepts and beliefs.

Thus do the two *mayas* share an identity of non-difference (*samatajnana*). Relatively they differ. Ultimately they are the same.

Great 14th century *Dzogchen* master Longchenpa bespeaks in his lapidary *Gyuma Galso* the inherent nondual *unitarity* (an apropos neologism of Niels Bohr) of the two *mayas*. How is this so?

There are two kinds/aspects of human ignorance. The first is inborn and innate. The other is learned. Innate ignorance is instinctive; we are born with it. It is the instinctual evolutionary view of self-ego-I, a perceiving subject inherently separate from all "other" selves and objects. It has proven most useful in allowing our species to dodge predators, both animal and human. The second face of ignorance is learned ignorance, the cognitive product of sociocultural conditioning—in Western culture our Greek materialist cognitive efflorescence that has become the destructive prevailing cognitive deep cultural background mass mind ideology of Scientific Materialism/Physicalism that has colonized the Western heart and mind. Both of these sad forms of ignorance (*avidya, marigpa*) are woefully short on altruistic kindness and compassion.

Dualistically appearing *avidya maya* experience is embraced and pervaded by the nondual *vidya maya* of the primordial "groundless ground" of being itself. As mere concepts both of these *mayas* are illusory. This unity of the inherently apparitional two *mayas* arises to our experience from the nondual "primordial purity" of the aboriginal emptiness ground/base (*gzhi rigpa*) in whom all appearing reality arises and is instantiated—perfectly free and unencumbered by desire, or by conceptual reification, fabrication, and elaboration. Because, in the *Perfect Sphere of Dzogchen*, our illusory and delusory realities are, in this Ultimate Truth view, "primordially pure" and undefiled "from the very beginning" all appearing *avidya maya* is "perfect just as it is". In the clear words of Gautama the Buddha:

> What you are is what you have been;
> What you will be is what you do now....
> So let it be as it is, and rest your weary mind;
> All things are perfect exactly as they are.

Yet, under sway of ignorance (*avidya*), and delusion (*moha*) we almost immediately conceptually interpret this selfless pristine pre-conceptual direct attentional/perceptual experience as afflictive emotional experience—sense desire, fear/anger, greed/pride, paralyzing doubt, and the rest. The result is human suffering. The antidote is instant effortless, spontaneous non-meditation—"placement of attention/awareness"—again and again upon our always present Buddha mind Presence, by whatever name or concept. *OM AH HUM PHAT!*

This is the foundation of timeless, radical nondual *Dzogchen* View and practice.

Further, this instant, always already present open "pure presence" of the original ground are at once both origin and aim of the cognitively fluent ambulant *Dzogchen* practitioner. "The ground is no different at the pinnacle of enlightenment than it is at the primordial base" (Adzom Rinpoche).

Caveat Auditor: Nonetheless, from the relative view, delusory dualistic *avidya maya* has a thorny thicket of bogus cognitive concepts on offer for the naively innocent obsessively thinking mind. *Avidya maya* concept-mind is a trickster. Don't be fooled. Please avoid impetuous true-false reality judgments based in our habitual, skeptical, dualistic deep cultural background "global web of belief" about what is true or false; good or bad.

Yet, wonder of wonders, it is this duplicitous, dualistic concept-mind of our very own self-ego-I that reflexively recognizes *avidya maya* just as it is; ignorance, illusion, and delusion. That reflective reflexive awareness cognition is after all the first step in waking up to our selfless, luminous, clear light love-wisdom mind Presence—primordial Buddha nature of mind—"supreme source" that is nothing less than our "supreme identity". Who am I? "That I Am!"—without a single exception.

Be That as it may, such complementary cognitive doublets may be—once the *ultimate* boundless love-wisdom wholeness ground (*jnana, yeshe*) in which they arise and abide is recognized/realized (*rtogs pa*)—useful gifts to our *relative* discriminating wisdom (*prajna*). *Prajna* facilitates spontaneous, skillful *bodhicitta* conduct—our thought, intention, and action for the benefit of living beings. And that after all is the Mahayana open secret of human happiness. The two wisdoms, ultimate and relative: Guru Rinpoche, Padmasambhava advises, "It is most important to practice these two as a unity".

Popular Buddhist idiom and ideology too often sees *Dzogchen* as a shortcut to *buddic* primordial awakening. Read some books about *Dzogchen trekchö* and *tögal* practice; rest occasionally in mostly conceptualized *rigpa;* maybe even show up for a *Yeshe Lama* weekend retreat; and become fully enlightened buddhas in this lifetime. But it is not so.

This great and precious *Dzogchen* wisdom treasure is decidedly not a conceptual enterprise. It cannot be learned, let alone accomplished through books, tapes, intellectual speculation, along with a bit of mindfulness practice. Indeed it cannot be learned at all. Buddha told, "This cannot be taught". The nondual primordial wisdom state of *Dzogchen* must be introduced to the prepared aspirant *directly*, non-conceptually, by the *Dzogchen* master. Yet, study and quiescent *shamatha* "taming the wild horse of the mind"—gathering our scattered "monkey mind"—is a propitious beginning.

Although, as we have just seen, the luminous Presence of *dynamic intrinsic awareness* that is the very Buddha nature of mind abides always present in our *ordinary mind stream*—and while the Great Perfection with its nondual *Ati Yoga* is indeed a direct and expedited path to ultimate awakening to our already present innate clear light *rigpa* love-wisdom Buddha mind Presence—*Dzogchen* practice requires assiduous "gradualist" contemplative, behavioral, ethical conduct preparation under the guidance of a qualified *Dzogchen* master. Only then shall be revealed the trans-conceptual miracle that "it is already accomplished from the very beginning". Should you aspire to such an ultimate path, please consider well this truth of *Dzogchen* practice: Garab Dorje's *Three Vajra Verses*:

> The nature of mind is Buddha from the beginning…
> Realizing the purity essence of all things, to remain

there without seeking is the meditation … .It is already
accomplished from the very beginning.

"To remain there without seeking is the meditation". That is
Dzogchen "non-meditation". Roughly speaking, in the Mahayana
Causal Vehicle, meditation seeks something—peace, happiness,
liberation from suffering, enlightenment. Practice this cause now,
and get that payoff later, in some blissful future mind state. In the
Dzogchen Fruitional View there is nothing to seek, and nothing to
accomplish. That which we seek is always already present. Seeking
that which we already actually are to avoid suffering, is a form of
suffering. Thus do we make our present imperfect practice itself
the goal. And everything that we feel, think, and do is our present
practice—both on and off the cushion.

Thus is *Dzogchen* View and "non-meditation" practice—with
assiduous *shamatha* meditation practice—the nondual Great
Perfection/Completion of the dualistic preparation of the
Mahayana Causal Vehicle. Yet, without this urgent "development
stage" Mahayana Middle Way Madhyamaka practice there is no
auspicious entry into *Dzogchen*. The *Dzogchen ngöndro* foundational
practices are an auspicious, difficult beginning. Effortless *Dzogchen*
practice requires hard work preparation—both conceptual and
contemplative. Please consider this well.

So, first we learn basic mantra and deity practice, along with
mindful *shamatha* meditation. We learn to rest in this luminous spacious Presence of our Buddha mind emptiness ground that is the
Perfect Sphere of Dzogchen, in whom everything arises.

Gradually we begin to notice that our concepts *about* our
indwelling Buddha mind is more and more nondual direct contemplative experience *of* it. We notice our hitherto constant concern for self has subtly shifted toward concern for the well being
of others, even beyond immediate family, We notice that the inces-
sant chatter of the mind is infused with love-wisdom mind awareness. We begin to notice that this very subtle process—wonder of
wonders—makes us happy, not later but now. We find ourselves

offering thanks for the precious gift of our life, just as it is now. *Emaho!*

Now, with this enhanced capacity, and with the occasional "pointing out" instruction of the qualified *Dzogchen* master, we approach the nondual *Dzogchen* View with its inherent *bodhicitta*; and its "non-meditation" awareness continuity of the Buddha's wisdom of emptiness.

Padmasambhava, in *Natural Liberation*, speaks of foundational *Dzogchen shamatha*:

> Flawless shamatha is like an oil lamp that is unmoved by wind. Wherever the awareness is placed, it is unwaveringly present; awareness is vividly clear, without being sullied by laxity, lethargy, or dimness; wherever the awareness is directed, it is steady and sharply pointed; and unmoved by adventitious thoughts, it is straight. Thus, a flawless meditative state arises in one's mind-stream; and until this happens, it is important that the mind is settled in its natural state … Cast your gaze downward, gently release your mind, and without having anything on which to meditate, gently release both your body and mind into their natural state … Without any modification or adulteration, place your attention simply without wavering, in its own natural state, its natural limpidity, its own character, just as it is now. Remain in clarity, and rest the mind so that it is loose and free … Fine stability will arise and you may even identify (primordial wisdom) awareness. (trans. Alan Wallace 1998. See *Appendix A* below.)

In *Dzogchen shamatha* practice, naturally arising discursive thoughts, mental images, and emotions—negative or positive—are not seen as troublesome distractions to reject or enjoy. Rather, one sees them as emanations or manifestations of *dharmakaya*, primordially pure and of the same nature as the vast expanse of the ground itself, just as waves are of the same nature as the great ocean.

Dzogchen is generally considered by those who know to be the most direct path to the final nondual realization of our ultimate Buddha nature—primordial "groundless ground" of all arising phenomenal reality, the very nature of mind and all its experience—perceptual, conceptual, contemplative, and nondual (*advaya*; "not one, not two").

Self and all arising spacetime phenomenal reality—our beloved "real world out there" (RWOT)—are thereby dynamic, luminous, empty virtual displays of the play of the mind observing this boundless whole—primordial awareness-consciousness ground itself in which, or in whom all our physical and mental experience is instantiated. We are luminous instances of That! It is told that resting naturally in this vast spacious boundless whole (*dharmadhatu*) is the primary cause of human happiness, both relative flourishing, and the liberation from suffering that is Happiness Itself. And "Wonder of wonders", "It is already accomplished from the very beginning", deep within us. It is that love wisdom mind to which we awaken as we tread the Buddhist Path.

Now, as to our open question, "How shall I know, and feel this?" *Shamatha* and *vipashyana* meditation practice open the gate to the path of the innermost esoteric *Dzogchen* Great Completion of the exoteric Buddhist Causal Vehicle—always under the guidance of the *Dzogchen* master.

Nyingma *Dzogchen* Master Dudjom Rinpoche clarifies this for us:

> (*Dzogchen*), which makes the result into the path is superior to the vehicle of the transcendental perfections which makes the cause into the path (*Nyingma School of Tibetan Buddhism*, Vol. I)

Thus is the ultimate Result or Fruit of enlightenment—our fully realized innate, primordial nondual wisdom *bodhi* Buddha mind (*jnana, yeshe*) that is realized as Buddhahood—taken as the "innermost" esoteric foundation of the tantric Path. Why? Because the result, Buddha nature/Buddha mind is always already present within us. So we work with that ultimate reality, from the outset. As Guru Rinpoche told, "We discover ultimate truth only by way of relative truth. Practice these as a unity". Meanwhile, "Keep your view as high as the sky; and your deeds as fine as barley flour."

In short, we "keep the view" that we are always already Buddha. Perhaps we are not yet fully awakened Buddhas, but we place our attention, moment to moment, upon our "supreme identity"—clear light Presence of our already present Buddha mind. That is the nondual original nature of mind—this wondrous gift of our here now present relative spacetime embodied, ultimately non-existent, cognizant, primordially pure and empty mind. Realizing That, we forget ourselves for a few moments and go to work to benefit living beings. It is That that makes us happy now. That is the teaching of the Buddha.

Once again, no need to seek happiness in some future perfect time or place, or mind state. Rather, we gradually awaken, through the assiduous practice of the Path, to that "supreme source" that we already are. Now present Presence of That. Who am I? To rehearse the Vedic pith, *Tat Tvam Asi*. That I Am! "It is already accomplished from the very beginning" (Garab Dorje). As Gautama Shakyamuni told so long ago, "Wonder of wonders, all beings are Buddha". Thus do we "Make the goal the path."

Conversely, the exoteric, dualistic sutra Mahayana Causal Vehicle (the dialectical vehicle) takes causality, cause and effect—practice these Six Perfections now and become a Buddha later—as the foundation of the Path. The main point here is that, although we are not yet fully awakened Buddhas, we are already Buddha! Our ordinary mind is Buddha mind from the very beginning! It is that great nondual Ultimate Truth to which we gradually awaken through the assiduous relative practice of the Path. This great Vajrayana tantric foundational premise makes all the difference in establishing the correct conceptual View (*darshana, lta ba*) from the outset. Who am I? I am Buddha from the very beginning. Good to know in approaching the *Dzogchen* Path, or at any stage of the Path (*marga, lam*); especially at the beginning.

Thus it is said, *Dzogchen Ati Yoga* is the teaching pinnacle, subtlest and "highest" view and practice of Nyingma "inner tantras", and the very Fruitional Vehicle of the entire buddhadharma Path.

While the causal Paramitayana and the fruitional Tibetan Vajrayana are equally concerned to "accomplish" Buddhahood, unlike the skillful objective conceptual means of Sutrayana, the tantras of highest *Ati Yoga Dzogchen* of the tantric vehicle has the benefit of subjective, trans-conceptual, innermost esoteric skillful means, to wit: highly efficacious, even blissful direct and innate clear light wisdom (*jnana, yeshe, gnosis*), and mantra and deity practice meditation under the direct empowering guidance of a qualified *Dzogchen* master; and in the crucible of the loving *sangha* spiritual community. Such a practice program is said to expedite Buddhahood in several lifetimes, or if you're lucky, in this lifetime, over against "innumerable *kalpas*" of rebirth for even the superior Sutrayana practitioner. Not surprisingly, those who hold the View of the Great Perfection view it as the perfect Path.

This fruitional tantric distinction is perhaps the main difference between the more or less exoteric objective and dualistic conceptual dialectics of the Sutrayana (*Sautrantika*) vehicle, and the esoteric Tantrayana/Vajrayana (Mantrayana) with its Middle Way Madhyamaka Prasangika teaching, the foundation of innermost esoteric, monistic panpsychic/cosmopsychic nondual *Dzogchen* view and praxis (*Appendix C*).

We shall soon see that in the View of the Great Perfection the *essence* (*kadag*) of all appearing physical and mental spacetime reality is boundless *shunyata*/emptiness. But emptiness is not merely a negative void because its *nature* is spontaneous presence (*lhundrub*), fullness of radiant luminosity (*prabhasa, 'od gsal*). Its *energy* is the manifested spontaneous expression in time and space of boundless compassion (*karuna, thugs re*)—great cosmic gift (*jinlob, euengelion*) of absolute *bodhicitta* whence arises the two relative *bodhicittas* of aspiration, and of action. Essence/*kadag*; nature/*lhundrub*; energy as compassion/*karuna*. It is compassionate *bodhicitta* that is our secret of human happiness.

These three conceptual faces—essence, nature, energy—of the Perfect Sphere of *Dzogchen* are in all ways an omnipresent, indivisible prior and present unity that is revealed through stabilized, nondual non-meditation of *Dzogchen Ati Yoga* practice.

Such are the things we must know when approaching the *Dzogchen* path

The Fundamental Innate Mind of Clear Light in Sutra and Tantra

Buddha told it well 25 centuries past,

> The mind is devoid of mind,
> for the nature of mind is clear light.

H.H. Dalai Lama (2000) teaches that the whole spectrum of Buddhist philosophy, ethics, and practice may be understood in terms of this one famous verse of the Buddha.

The first line presents the wisdom of the First Turning of the Wheel of Dharma (the *dharmachakra*), the teaching of the Four Noble Truths, and the entire meaning of Buddhist Sutrayana—of emptiness/*shunyata*, and of *bodhicitta*. The first line also introduces the wisdom of Mahayana Middle Way Madhyamaka, the Second Turning of the Wheel of the Buddha's Teaching.

The second line of the verse—"for the nature of mind is clear light"—encompasses the meaning of the Third Turning of the Wheel, namely, Buddha's teaching on our innate indwelling Buddha nature (*tathagatagarbha*)/Buddha mind (*buddhadhatu, buddhajnana*), the nondual primordial innate clear light Buddha nature of mind. The nondual *Ati Yoga* of *Dzogchen*, the Great Completion, is the practice of accomplishing this fundamental "innate mind of clear light"—non-conceptual, pristine, naked, essential Buddha mind-stream, our indwelling open Presence of That!

For His Holiness, clear light mind nature may be understood at two levels, the Mahayana sutra teaching system, and the Vajrayana tantra teaching system. When the clear light nature of mind is understood in terms of both of these together there are two distinct references: 1) the "emptiness of the mind" which corresponds to the "objective clear light", and 2) "the essential cognizant luminous clarity and awareness" of the very nature of mind itself, which corresponds to the "subjective experience of clear light". In the clear words of H.H. Dalai Lama:

> The fundamental innate mind of clear light is considered to be the nature of mind, or the ultimate root of consciousness... This is the same experience to which Mahamudra leads, to which Dzogchen leads, and to which the union of clarity and emptiness (Sakya) leads... If you analyse them, they all arrive at the same point... As soon as there is clear and aware consciousness it is said to be permeated by the clear light rigpa... indwelling clear light, essential rigpa... When this aware aspect of rigpa is directly introduced and recognized, it can be identified even in the very thick of arising thoughts... In Dzogchen, while thoughts are active, rigpa permeates them all, so that even at the very moment when powerful thoughts like attachment and aversion are arising, there remains a pervasive quality of clear light rigpa. That rigpa you make into your practice
> —H.H. Dalai Lama, *Dzogchen*, 2000, p 168 ff

High Dharma in a Cold Climate: *Dzogchen* View and Practice

In the ancient Nyingma tradition of Vajrayana Tibetan Buddhism *Dzogchen* (*Dzogpachenpo*, Skt. *Mahasandi*) is seen as the definitive, highest teaching of Gautama Shakyamuni Buddha—the "innermost secret" teaching that he taught only to disciples of the greatest capacity and most assiduous preparation.

We've seen that the *Dzogchen* (*Dzog;* complete or perfect; *chen,* great) teaching is said to have arisen from Samantabhadra (Tib. Kuntazangpo), primordial formless *dharmakaya Adi Buddha* in whom all spacetime reality form arises and appears. The teaching was then directly transmitted to Vajrasattva, *Adi Buddha* of the *sambhogakaya* dimension of light-form; then from Vajrasattva to the human *nirmanakaya* Garab Dorje (d. 55 C.E.), who recorded it for his disciple Manjushrimitra, who then classified it into the three *Dzogchen* teaching cycles—*semde, longde,* and secret *mengagde* or *upadesha.* This was then passed on to his disciple Shrisimha, then to Jnanasutra, and then in the 8th century to Tibet via Vimalamitra and Padmasambhava. In the 14th century "the omniscient" Longchen Rabjam or Longchenpa (1308-1364) synthesized the great teaching into a unified teaching Path. Jigme Lingpa (1730-1798) edited it into its present form as the *Longchen Nyingthig.* (For a more detailed history please see *Appendix B*: "A Brief History of the *Dzogchen* Transmission".)

We've seen that for Nyingma school, the traditional three extant Buddhist teaching vehicles—Hinayana/Theravada, Mahayana, and Vajrayana—have become the *Nine Vehicles* to liberation from suffering and the ultimate clear light full *bodhi* awakening to our already present Buddha mind (*buddhajnana*). That propitious Result is buddhahood itself.

H.H. Dalai Lama teaches that the first eight of these Nine Vehicles of Nyingma utilize our reflective, relative conventional ordinary obstructed mind working as the cause and effect Mahayana Causal Vehicle to accomplish the ultimate full *bodhi* enlightenment of buddhahood. The bad news: it is said that such a path of renunciation and transformation takes countless lifetimes.

We have also seen that in the *Dzogchen* Resultant or Fruitional Vehicle ordinary mind itself is recognized as already "primordially pure" Buddha mind "from the very beginning". This subtle, direct supreme vehicle—the *Ati Yoga* of *Dzogchen*, the nondual Great Perfection or Great Completion of the dualistic Mahayana Causal Vehicle—utilizes our already present indwelling dynamic intrinsic primordial awareness wisdom itself as the Path. And yes, this path is considered by most Vajrayana masters to be the pinnacle—with Essence Mahamudra—of all the Buddhist teaching vehicles, and may, under the most auspicious circumstances, be "accomplished" in a single lifetime. That's the good news.

This primordial awareness wisdom is the constant and "unchang-ing *rigpa* awareness" that is not other than Samantabhadra, pri-mordial *Adi Buddha* of the all embracing aboriginal *dharmakaya* reality dimension. This *dharmakaya* Buddha is the "Supreme Source" (*Kenjed Gyalpo*), and represents our pristine fundamental nature, the "fundamental innate mind of clear light". It is utterly "primordially pure" and untainted by the karmic winds of dualistic conceptual thought and negative emotion and action.

In *Dzogchen* View and Practice luminous, numinous primordial awareness wisdom Presence—*rigpa, vidya*—is inherently present in all human beings, without a single exception. It is not something that happens conditionally—if we're good, kind, and helpful. Instant open Presence is already the case. Indeed it is who we actu-ally are now.

Moreover, all of the physical and mental phenomena of relative spacetime reality arise, participate, and pass away within this vast unbounded primordial whole, by whatever name or concept. All arising reality is imbued with this primordial Buddha nature (*tatha-gatagarbha*). Just so, that same primordial essence is the "supreme identity" of each and every human being—bright compassionate Presence of That. On the accord of H.H. Dalai Lama:

The most important way to understand the Great Perfection is in terms of essence, nature and compassionate energy according to which the essence is primordial purity (*kadag*) and the nature is spontaneous presence (*lhundrub*)... All the phenomena of samsara and nirvana and the path are, by their very nature, the *rigpa* awareness that is the primordial buddha Samantabhadra, and they are never outside of the primordial expanse of buddhahood... This is the funda-mental innate mind of clear light.

—H.H. Dalai Lama, 2007, p. 78

In other words, according to 19th century Nyingma *Rimé* poly-math Ju Mipham:

Within the essence original wakefulness which is primordially pure (*kadag*) manifests the nature, a radiance which is spontaneously present (*lhundrub*).

Thus it is, in the *Dzogchen* view, the fundament of clear light ground luminosity is the *Trikaya of the Base* or the three Buddha bodies—*dharmakaya, sambhogakaya, nirmanakaya*—that is our "supreme source" (*cittadhatu, kunjed gyalpo*), ultimate reality itself (*dharmata, cho-nyid*), the very nature of mind (*sems-nyid, buddhi*): its *essence* is emptiness/*shunyata*; its *nature* is luminous clarity (*gsal-ba*); its *energy* continuously emanates as the compassionate *kosmic* gift (*jinlob*) of *ultimate bodhicitta* that is our home as guests of this spacetime phenomenal dimension of light/motion/form (*tsal, rolba, $E=mc^2$*).

This *jnana prana* wisdom energy naturally, selflessly expresses itself in human conduct as *relative bodhicitta*—compassionate wisdom (*thugs re*)—the thought, intention, and action to benefit living beings. Herein abides our own true happiness as individual/social beings.

Therefore, the infinite, empty boundless vast expanse of basic space (*chos ying*) that is the unborn, uncreated, unbounded whole (*dharmadhatu*) is our nondual ultimate reality ground itself—Ultimate Truth (*paramartha satya*)—*dharmakaya*. From that unbroken whole interdependently arises (*pratitya samutpada*) relative form—Relative Truth (*samvriti satya*) from its ultimate emptiness "groundless ground". As Buddha told, "Form is empty; emptiness is form. Form is not other than emptiness; emptiness is not other than form."

Our Four Human Cognitive Dimensions
Ultimately considered, the Buddha's complementary Two Truths—Relative and Ultimate—of the vast formless primordial unbounded whole itself are recognized, then realized as a *one truth* prior and present unity. That utterly nondual unified one truth is invariant throughout our entire human awareness-consciousness processional—perceptual, conceptual, contemplative, and nondual.

The phenomenological pie of human experience of the appearing physical and mental forms of reality may be sliced in several different ways. Indeed, noetic (body, mind, spirit integration/unity) philosopher Ken Wilber has established his prodigious integral philosophy upon such human cognitive states and stages (Wilber 2006, 2017).

The following section represents what I intend to be an integral, essential, simplified schema of the four dimensional world of human cognitive formation and experience. The Reader may wish to add a few strata, or reduce the whole shebang to one or two cognitive dimensions.

I have for the sake of simplicity glossed over important differences between *cognitive states* and *life stages*. Cognitive states do not neatly map onto life stages resulting in a bit of intellectual untidiness. Broadly construed, cognitive states are attentionally fluent and nonlocal—here now experience. Life stages have location and duration in sociocultural space and time. Nonlocal cognitive states much less so.

Evolutionary individual life *stages* are constituted in part by our present dominant cognitive *states* which condition and inform them; and in which we live for a period in time. In this way do the cognitive states upon which we *choose*—consciously or not—to place our attentional awareness define the phenomenal world in which we live. *Awareness management: From the cognitive states you choose arises the life world you deserve.*

For example, the waking consciousness of a professional theoretical physicist may be engaged primarily in cognitive state 2)—objective/conceptual (see below). As he/she is perhaps cognitively biased against entering spooky contemplative state 3), that mind state remains taboo, and closed. Still, incursions into state 3) occur during petitionary prayer, deep dreamless sleep, and the *kosmic* bliss of playing with the grandkids. Still, our physicist abides for a time in a life stage defined by mostly state 2) objective cognition.

Now, the Tibetan Buddhist Lama and *Dzogchen* master whose on-campus teaching our scholarly physicist decides to attend due in no small part to curiosity arising from a stage 3) recurring dream about preachers in red robes—that Lama abides mainly in state/ stage 4)—the prior all-subsuming unity of a continuity of experience of all four cognitive states at once.

That very "advanced" Lama can dwell in the luminous mindstream of all the Buddhas in early morning prayer and meditation; jog on a treadmill at noon; engage formidable ontological conceptual Buddhist dialectics in the afternoon; teach students at any and all levels of understanding in the evening; and sleep four hours at night, while never departing state 4) cognition. Such a one abides mainly in a life world state we might call nondual life stage 4).

Should our physicist choose to establish a cognitive state 3) contemplative practice with our life stage 4) Lama; and as he/she enters the primordial love-wisdom mindstream of the Lama, that person may indeed, in due course, enter a subtler, perhaps happier life stage, namely, state/stage 3).

Let us now further consider the four mind states of our human cognitive evolutionary capacity.

Our four cognitive dimensional states: 1) Pre-conceptual ordinary direct perception, prior to conceptual imputation, reification, and naming. 2) Exoteric, dualistic, objective, conceptual cognition. We spend most of our waking lives here. 3) Esoteric, subjective, mostly non-conceptual contemplative cognition (meditation). 4) "Innermost secret" perfectly subjective nondual cognition—beyond the subject-object split—timeless, buddic, direct yogic perception (yogi pratyaksa) and complete cognitive rest in the nature of mind.

As to evolutionary cognitive development, each ascending cognitive state transcends and embraces the previous state. For example, post-empirical state 3) understands and includes perceptual state 1) and conceptual empirical state 2); but not the utterly trans-conceptual nondual subtlety of state 4) experience—like the mother's loving embrace of the mind of her child, but not the other way round.

Ascending human evolution through this multi-dimensional awareness-consciousness continuum beyond or above state 2) is largely a function—always with our compassionate *bodhicitta*—of our ongoing attentional awareness commitment to state 3), which perforce, in due course and by grace, opens the heart and mind into the nondual clear light luminosity of state 4). Clearly, recognizing and entering in the *Perfect Sphere of Dzogchen* is a stage 4) post-empirical, non-logocentric act of nondual state 4) cognition.

Moreover, early in state/stage 3) the requested intervention of a qualified meditation master is required to "introduce" via direct spiritual transmission the prepared aspirant to his/her own "self-perfected state of *Dzogchen*"—"innermost secret" wisdom mind *buddic* Presence; and to tame and guide the egocentric "wild horse" of the student's mind through its prodigious mostly unconscious cognitive biases, excuses, and ego-defensive strategies of avoidance of psycho-emotional-spiritual growth.

A secure, stable, intelligent and cognitively fluent ego-I is required by the student for the process to bear fruit. *lama khyen.* The Lama/Guru mirrors to the student his/her own innermost Lama/Guru. "Lama walks with Loma". But what self-respecting secure and intelligent ego-I with intellectual or spiritual "success" at state/stage 2) desires to become a student again? You can see the problem. Yes. It takes a bit of humility, and courage.

Although these four cognitive states appear linear in time, the Buddhas, *mahasiddhas*, sages and saints of our Primordial Wisdom Tradition—embodied or not—who abide in the unity of the timeless and eternal dimension of state/stage 4) experience all four states more or less simultaneously and continuously as a nondual prior and present unity. This is then the potential of the practitioner at any level.

Yes, the perfect "self-perfected state of *Dzogchen*"is always already present and awake at the Heart of the human being. But it takes a bit of guided practice to awaken the untrained mind to realization of that great truth.

Just so, practitioners at state 3)—upon entering in ever so briefly our state 4) nondual state of Presence (*rigpa, vidya*)—also experience all four cognitive states at once. As state 3) established practice begins to stabilize the hitherto untrained distracted mind, we connect as we will, "brief moments, many times", to the peace and the yogi's bliss of lucid state 4) awakening. All of the Buddhas and *mahasiddhas* of the three times—past, present, future—have told of this multi-dimensional awakening process.

Clearly, the wondrous, sometimes scintillating human conceptual virtuosity of state 2) in no way exhausts the many mansions of this great whole that is our intrinsic human intelligence. That it does, demonstrates the inherent, natural cognitive bias of state 2). Our collective sociocultural life *stages* are an out-picturing of our individual cognitive *states*.

The pragmatic and wonderfully productive Western scientific paradigm—Scientific Materialism—may well be the pinnacle of state/stage 2) development. The ΛCDM (lambda cold dark matter) Standard Model of Physics and Cosmology with its relativistic quantum electrodynamics (QED) is arguably the greatest *intellectual* achievement of humankind.

Yet, such valorization and idealization of Science has a cost. We have seen that the price paid for this obsessively objective/conceptual habit of mind is the colonization of Western mind and culture by the monolithic monistic metaphysic of Scientific Materialism/Physicalism. The unhappy result is a profound materialist/physicalist deep background cultural bias—our materialist/physicalist "global web of belief" (Quine 1969). This problematic global cognitive bias closes William Blake's "doors of perception" to subtler or higher state/stage 3) and state/stage 4) human cognition. Buddhist philosopher-practitioner Alan Wallace has labeled this sad mind-state of affairs the "taboo of subjectivity". The destructive effect represents a profound cognitive limit upon human happiness—psychological, emotional, and spiritual.

The good news? Humanity now dwells upon the cusp of our next global knowledge paradigm—the 21st century integral Noetic Revolution in Matter, Mind, and Spirit that is now upon us (Boaz 2021b). Our collective human consciousness now bestrides an uneasy cognitive gap between the self-satisfied naïveté of state/ stage 2) and state/stage 3) which transcends and includes 2).

Just as our four cognitive states are an ultimate unity, the Buddhist Two Truths—Relative and Ultimate—share a relation of identity. How is this so? The all inclusive nondual formless dimension of Ultimate Truth—non-conceptually cognized at state/stage 4)—embraces, subsumes, and pervades the dynamic dualistic space-time form dimension of Relative Truth (state/stages 1, 2, 3) arising therein. Just so, cognitive state/stage 4) transcends yet embraces the less inclusive first three cognitive states and respective stages.

It is our always already present open awareness Presence (*vidya*, *rigpa*)—fully present to that *ultimate* primordial wholeness ground state (*gzhi rigpa*)—that knows and feels the truth of this great unified reality process. The practice of the Path with the living *Dzogchen* master and the *sangha* spiritual community opens the heart and mind of the yogi and yogini to receive the love, wisdom and deep inner ease and peace of it. And that is the very secret of both relative and ultimate human happiness. Pragmatic soteriology indeed.

Great 14th century *Dzogchen* master Gyalwa Longchen Rabjam (Longchenpa, 1308-1364), synthesizer of the entire previous *Dzogchen* wisdom transmission (*Appendix B*) speaks of this, our conceptually unelaborated, "innermost secret" state of awareness Presence of the great unbounded whole itself. Longchenpa's homage to the "primordial purity" of awareness state 4):

Naturally occurring timeless awareness—utterly lucid awakened mind—is marvelous and superb, primordially and spontaneously present. It is the treasury from which comes the universe of appearances and possibilities, whether samsara or nirvana. Homage to the unwavering state, free of conceptual elaboration.

—Treasury of the Basic Space of Phenomena (2001)

Please consider Longchenpa's mind to mind transmission to us of this primordial awareness love-wisdom (*jnana*, *yeshe*, *gnosis*), the "fundamental innate mind of clear light", the very Buddha nature (*tathagatagarbha*) of mind (*citatta, sems nyid*), *dharmakaya* emptiness ground of the great whole of all our arising realities (*dharmata, cho nyid*):

> Self arising wisdom is *rigpa* that is empty, clear and free from all conceptual elaboration, like an immaculate sphere of crystal ... It does not analyze objects ... By simply identifying that non-conceptual, pristine, naked *rigpa*, you realize there is nothing other than this nature ... This is nondual self-arising wisdom ... Like a reflection in a mirror, when objects and perceptions manifest to *rigpa*, that pristine and naked awareness which does not proliferate into thought is called the inner power (*tsal*), the responsiveness that is the ground (*gzhi*) for all the arising of things ... For a yogin who realizes the naked meaning of *Dzogpachenpo, rigpa* is fresh, pure and naked, and objects may manifest and appear within *rigpa*, but it does not lose itself externally to those objects.
>
> —Longchen Rabjam, *Treasury of the Dharmadhatu* (Commentary), Adzom Chögar Ed.

The Supreme Source

What is perhaps the primary *Dzogchen* tantra, *The Kunjed Gyalpo (The Supreme Source)*, must surely be considered one of humankind's great spiritual treasures. According to 20th century *Dzogchen* master Chögyal Namkhai Norbu, this prehistorical supreme nondual teaching—by whatever name—has been transmitted from master to disciple directly, heartmind to heartmind, for thousands of years.

However, historical *Dzogchen* wisdom dates from the teaching of Garab Dorje (d. 55 CE), as we have seen. The *Kunjed Gyalpo* tantra arises in the 8th Century and is the fundamental tantra of the *Dzogchen semde* (mind) teaching cycle. This reading of the great nonlocal, nondual primordial *Dzogchen* teaching is derived from Buddhist Vajrayana/Tantrayana understanding of the ultimate clear light nature of mind, yet its truth essence runs like a golden thread through the grand tapestry of humankind's great nondual Primordial Wisdom Tradition.

Kunjed Gyalpo, The Wise and Glorious King is Samantabhadra (luminous clarity) and Samantabhadri (boundless emptiness) in inseparable *yab-yum* embrace—androgynous skylike primordial *Adi Buddha*—the union of luminous clarity and emptiness that is none other than our original Buddha nature, supreme source, basis, primordial womb of everything. Samantabhadra, formless *Dharmakaya* Buddha descends into the realm of light and speaks to the *Logos*, Vajrasattva, Buddha of the *Sambhogakaya* reality dimension:

> The essence of all the Buddhas exists prior to samsara and nirvana...it transcends the four conceptual limits and is intrinsically pure; this original condition is the uncreated nature of existence that has always existed, the ultimate nature of all phenomena...It is utterly free of the defects of dualistic thought which is only capable of referring to an object other than itself...it is the base of primordial purity...Similar to space it pervades all beings...The inseparability of the two truths, absolute and relative is called 'primordial Buddha'...If at the moment the energy of the base manifests, one does not consider it something other than oneself...it self-liberates...Understanding the essence...one finds oneself always in this state...dwelling in the fourth time, beyond past, present and future...the infinite space of self-perfection...pure dharmakaya, the essence of the vajra of clear light.
>
> —Chögyal Namkhai Norbu, 1999

Thus do the sutras and the tantras of Buddha's teaching, and all of the bivalent dualities and dialectics of the Buddhist path—objective-subjective, existence-nonexistence, form-emptiness, self-noself, observer-data, true-false, relative truth-ultimate truth—abide "utterly free of the defects of dualistic thought", in the prior unity of the interdependently arisen *Perfect Sphere of Dzogchen,* the Great

Perfection. This perfect all-embracing sphere of ultimate reality is nothing less than our ultimate *buddic* mind nature, luminous innate clear light wisdom mind that is always already the unity of awareness and emptiness, of clarity and emptiness, and of bliss and emptiness.

Who is it, that I am? All the Buddhas and *mahasiddhas* of the three times have told it. This infinite vast expanse of the primordial awareness wisdom tantric continuum, "supreme source", boundless all-inclusive whole itself—bright indwelling Presence of That—is who we actually are!

Recall our ancient Vedic locution, *Tat Tvam Asi.* That, I Am! *That* is our "supreme identity"—by any name—the *Dzogchen* Great Completion of our always present Buddha nature, deep heart-seed Presence of ultimate happiness that is both origin and aim of all our urgent, dualistic, happiness seeking strategies. All the wisdom masters of the three times have told it: that which we seek is already present, deep within us. Chögyal Namkhai Norbu on this primordial supreme source:

> In terms of the source, the root of all phenomena, there is no such thing as an observer and an object to observe. All the phenomena of existence, without exception, abide in the supreme source in a condition of birthlessness...As the supreme source, Samantabhadra, pure and total consciousness, I am the mirror in which all phenomena are reflected. Although lacking self-nature everything exists clearly; without need for a (conceptual) view, the nature shines clear. Understanding the essential unborn condition is not an object to observe dualistically. This is the great understanding!
>
> —Chögyal Namkhi Norbu, 1999

Basic Space: Our Innate Mind of Clear Light

Recent Tibetan *Dzogchen* ecumenical *Rimé* master Tulku Urgyen Rinpoche teaches that the two innermost principles of *Dzogchen*

are basic space (*dharmadhatu*, Tib. *chos ying*) and primordial awareness presence (*vidya, rigpa*). Basic space is fecund luminous boundless *shunyata*/emptiness, the innate clear light luminosity (*'od gsal*)
itself. In the *Dzogchen* View the "innermost secret" realization of
basic space is *klong*, infinite vast expanse of all embracing primordial reality itself, transcending any conceptual elaboration or limit,
judgment or bias, beyond even the subtlest subject-object duality,
beyond objective and subjective emptiness, beyond ground and
path luminosity.

> As space pervades, so awareness pervades...like space,
> rigpa is all-encompassing...Just as beings are all pervaded
> by space, rigpa pervades the minds of beings ....Basic space
> is the absence of mental constructs, while awareness is the
> knowing of this absence of constructs, recognizing the com-
> plete emptiness of mind essence...The ultimate dharma is
> the realization of the indivisibility of basic space and aware-
> ness (that is) Samantabhadra.
>   —Tulku Urgyen (*As It Is*, Vol. I, 1999,
>   and *Rainbow Painting*, 1995)

Therefore, basic space (*dharmadhatu, cho ying*) and primordial
awareness wisdom (*jnana, yeshe, gnosis*) are an indivisible prior
ontological, and present epistemological and phenomenal unity.
Emptiness and our innate clear light Buddha love-wisdom mind
share this *kosmic* nondual relation of identity.

On the accord of the Third Dodrupchen, Jigme Tenpe Nyima
(quoted in H.H. Dalai Lama *Dzogchen*, 2000): "The *rigpa* taught
in the Nyingma *Dzogchen* approach and the wisdom of clear light
(Kagyu and Gulug school *Mahamudra/Anuttara-yoga-tantra*) are one
and the same":

> In *Dzogchen*, on the basis of the clear light itself, the way in which
> the clear light abides is made vivid and certain by the aspect
> of *rigpa* or knowing. That is free of any overlay of delusion and

from any corrupting effect due to conceptual thoughts that will inhibit the experience of clear light...It is not accomplished as anything new, as a result of circumstances and conditions, but is present from the very outset...an awareness that can clearly perceive the way in which basic space and wisdom are present. On the basis of that key point, the realization of clear light radiates in splendor, becoming clearer and clearer, like a hundred million suns...Here the aware aspect of clear light or effulgent *rigpa* (arising from essential *rigpa*) is stripped bare and you penetrate further into the depths of clear light...even as objects seem to arise...It is on the basis of this that you train (your mind).

This poetry of the nondual *Dzogchen* View was beautifully expressed by a great Tang Dynasty Ch'an/Zen Chinese master who likely had never heard of *Dzogchen*. His name was Haung Po (d. 850 CE):

All the Buddhas and all sentient beings are nothing but the one mind, beside which nothing exists. The one mind alone is Buddha. There is no distinction between Buddha and sentient beings....This one pure mind, the source of all things, shines forever with the radiance of its own perfection...like the sun rising through empty sky illuminates the whole world...Still your mind and it is here....Human beings are attached to forms and so seek externally for Buddhahood. It is by this very seeking that they lose it (*Ch'uan-hsin Fa-yao).*

Lovely dharma poetry. Beautiful words indeed. And how shall we ordinary folks directly connect to and know this always already present Presence of our innermost clear light love-wisdom Buddha mind? How indeed. That is the question that the *AtiYoga* of *Dzogchen* answers directly—for those courageous souls who choose to engage it.

We first establish an effective "real practice" under the guidance of a qualified *Dzogchen* meditation master (*Appendix A*), and in the loving context of the *sangha* community. We must ask for direct transmission if we truly desire it. If we have already done this, we make the *goal* of this precious gift of all encompassing practice, not seeking enlightenment in some divine future mind state, but our ordinary, difficult everyday path itself—step by mindful step—"brief moments many times". This natural continuity of clear light love-wisdom awareness is already present deep within us, here now. It is That great trans-conceptual truth to which we awaken through the relationship of the Lama.

Verily, everything, all of our cognitive experience—physical, emotional, mental, and spiritual; objective, subjective, contemplative, and perfectly subjective nondual; every thought, intention, and action—is the practice of the Path. All of that is our already present Buddha mind Presence. Let it be so.

The Three Vajra Verses

Here are H.H. Dudjom Rinpoche's luminous Comments on Garab Dorje's *Three Vajra Verses* or *The Three Essential Points* that are the *Dzogchen* Base, View, Path, Meditation, Result, and Conduct (translated by John M. Reynolds):

Verse I: Recognize your own true nature—through direct introduction/transmission by the *Dzogchen* master (The Base/Ground and the View). "This fresh immediate awareness of the present moment, transcending all thoughts related to the three times (past, present, future), is itself that primordial awareness wisdom *(yeshe)* that is self-originated intrinsic awareness *(rig pa)*."

From this Base and View arises the *Dzogchen Semde* (mind) teaching cycle.

Verse II: Choose the state of presence, beyond doubt (The Path and Meditation). "Whatever phenomena of *samsara* or *nirvana* may manifest, all of it represents the play of the creative energy or potentiality of one's own immediate intrinsic awareness presence *(rig pa'i rtsal)*. One must decide upon this unique state for oneself, and know that there exists nothing other than this."

From This Path and Meditation arises the *Dzogchen Longde* (space) teaching cycle.

Verse III: Continue in the state with confidence in liberation (The Result and Conduct). "Whatever gross or subtle thoughts may arise, by merely recognizing their nature, they arise and self-liberate simultaneously in the vast expanse of *Dharmakaya*, where Emptiness and Awareness are nondual and inseparable *(gsal stong gnyis med)*."

From this Result and Conduct arises the *Dzogchen* "innermost secret" *Upadesha (Mengagde)*, or heart essence *(nyingthig)* teaching cycle.

The Six Vajra Verses of Vairochana.

These *Three Essential Points* (*The Three Vajra Verses*) of the essence, nature and energy of the Base, and of the Path, and of the Fruition/Result is contained in *Dhyani* Buddha Vairochana's early *Dzogchen* tantra, the *Six Vajra Verses*, or "Cuckoo of the State of Presence" (*Rig-pa'I khu-byug*), luminous Buddha mind Presence (*vidya, rigpa*) of intrinsic awareness that each human being is.

The cuckoo is the sacred bird of *Bönpo* founder Shenrab Miwo and is considered in the aboriginal *Bön* tradition as the king of birds, harbinger of spring and bearer of the primordial wisdom from vast empty space of *dharmakaya*. These early *Six Vajra Verses* of Vairochana, and the hundreds of *Dzogchen* tantras and texts that issue from it are but commentaries on Garab Dorje's above *Three Vajra Verses* or *The Three Essential Statements* (*The Three Points That Strike the Essence*).

The Six Vajra Verses (translated by Chögyal Namkhai Norbu):

Verse 1 & 2: The Base (View): The nature of phenomena is non-dual (*gnyis med*), and each one, its own state, is beyond the limits of the mind (*Dzogchen semde* or mind meditation cycle).

Verse 3 & 4: The Path, Way of Practice (Meditation): There is no concept that can define the condition of "what is," but vision nevertheless manifests: all is good (*Dzogchen longde*, or space meditation cycle).

Verse 5 & 6: The Fruit, Result, Way of Being in Action (Conduct): Everything has already been accomplished, and so, having overcome the sickness of effort (spiritual seeking), one finds oneself in the self-perfected state: (*Dzogchen mengagde/upadesha*, or secret essence meditation cycle).

And from 18th century *Dzogchen* master Jigme Lingpa—great unifier of Longchenpa's syncretic corpus, and author of the *Longchen Nyingthig: Heart Essence of the Vast Expanse*—on the nondual Great Perfection *Dzogchen* view:

> No Buddhas, no beings, beyond existence and non-existence intrinsic awareness itself is absolute Guru—Ultimate Truth. By resting naturally, beyond fixation in that inherently free perfect innate *Bodhi mind*, I take refuge and actualize Bodhicitta.
>
> —Jigme Lingpa, *Longchen Nyingthig*

"The perfect explanation of *Dzogchen*", according to Chögyal Namkhai Norbu is voiced in these perfect words of Gautama, our historical *Nirmanakaya* Buddha:

> All that arises is essentially no more real than a reflection, transparently pure and clear, beyond all definition or logical explanation.
>
> Yet the seeds of past action, karma, continue to cause further arising. Even so, know that all that exists is ultimately devoid of self-nature, utterly nondual.

Nondual Non-Meditation: Undistracted Ordinary Mind

Please consider this: In the luminous, numinous space between, and within, and throughout our relative perceptions, thoughts, feelings and beliefs already abides our ultimate primordial innate clear light love-wisdom mind—profound innermost Presence of That. Connect to That, moment to moment. Mindful mantra wisdom breath (*pranajnana*) is the skillful method. *OM AH HUM*. That is the great happiness *Dzogchen* teaching.

We've often seen in these pages that our Buddha mind Presence is transpersonal/trans-ego, non-conceptual and trans-rational; that is, it utterly transcends our deep cultural background realist/materialist "scientific" paradigm,—our reality constituting Western "global web of belief" as to its objective existence or nonexistence. Yet, our Buddha mind is always right here now, upon each mantra breath! Even when we forget. All the masters of the three times have told it: your *bodhi* mind wisdom mind Presence is always already present! But don't *believe* this. It's beyond belief. As Buddha told, "Come and see".

Undistracted Ordinary Mind. In the most subtle nondual view and practice of Vajrayana *Dzogchen,* and of definitive Essence *Mahamudra,* mindfulness meditation practice is already simply present now in "undistracted ordinary mind"; the "primordially pure" natural "self-perfected state" of spontaneously aware Presence— conceptually empty luminous awareness that is always present right here and now, in the midst of all kinds of thinking, feeling, and physical distractions. "Without past, present, future; empty awake mind" (Ju Mipham).

This nondual, innermost esoteric teaching on the nondual primordial nature of mind unfolds "from the top" as the "immediacy of the View", while the dualistic Path ascends from below. Guru Rinpoche, Padmasambhava teaches: "Keep your view as high as the sky; and your deeds as fine as barley flour … It is most important to practice these two as a unity."

Thus is confidence and certainty of the *View* established through the nondual *Meditation,* and the compassionate *Conduct* of the *Path*: View, Meditation, and Conduct/Action.

Recall the *Dzogchen Three Vajra Verses*: 1) Recognize your own true nature (via direct introduction/transmission from the *Dzogchen* master); 2) Choose the state of Presence beyond doubt; 3) Continue in the state with confidence in liberation". That is the already self-perfected unity of *Dzogchen* View and Meditation.

As Lord Buddha's teaching enters the West the immediacy of the nondual View, along with the Lama's "pointing out instruction" is introduced directly by some Vajrayana Tibetan Lamas at the beginning of the process of the Path, before the student's accomplishment of the daunting preliminary practices of *ngöndro*, and "development stage" practice, which may or may not be done later as the View and Path become more established, and the unruly mind more stabilized. Why do *Dzogchen* Lamas do this?

A basic working understanding of the View—and the profound relative, conventional everyday peace and happiness that arises from it—is always here now, from the very beginning! Our immediate happiness is already present! Happiness—bright Presence of That—is already the case. It is not at all dependent upon later "advanced practice". Human happiness is always right here now in our *undistracted ordinary mind*. It follows the *pranajnana* wind of mantra breath. We simply breathe consciously and open the heart and the mind to receive it, this eternal present moment now. That is the simple miracle of radical, "self-perfected" *Dzogchen* truth. Jesus the Christ has told it well: "That which you seek is already present within you; and it is spread out upon the face of the earth, but you do not see it" (*Luke* 17). Now we can see it.

So, having direct happy experience of Presence, we gradually learn to manage distractions. That is the *Dzogchen* View. There is no need to believe this. Ultimately, it is just more words. And it is assuredly beyond belief. Thus do we open to receive it *directly* (*yogi pratyaksa*). As Buddha told so long ago, "O monks, do not believe what I teach out of respect for me. Come and see."

That said, we must, through the Buddha's basic "mindfulness of breathing", and with basic mantra prayer (*OM AH HUM*) begin to "bracket" our deep cultural background skepticism and doubt—our dubious materialist "global web of belief"—and open our heart-mind to receive. That is how we manage the natural endless painful distractions.

But the goal is not to block or to end the distractions. The goal is not to end life's inevitable adversity. Adversity happens! It's how we *choose* to respond that matters; is it not? So once again, we simply connect to our already present Presence—moment to moment—through mindful mantra breath. Anxiety, impatience, and harsh judgementalism lose a bit of their power. We learn to go easy on and forgive ourselves, and through this we forgive others—especially those we love most.

We've seen that the outer and inner seeking strategies for such happiness doesn't work. So, we stop seeking and simply relax into, and then rest in our already present love-wisdom mind Presence—"brief moments, many times". Our relief need not be some mystical "advanced practice". Our immediate touchstone is here upon the mindful mantra breath—our ongoing instant connection to that.

Hot Tip! If you have not already done so, get a Lama in your life. If you have done so, remember again and again that you are always already now that Lama/Guru Presence. The outer Guru always mirrors your inner Guru. Bright Presence of That. "Lama walks always with *loma*".

Most surprising to our concepts and beliefs *about* the path of meditation—with the introduction by the Lama of *undistracted ordinary mind* to the prepared "ripe" student—there is no need to change anything! No need to seek some paradigmatic ideal "perfect meditation", or contemplative accomplishment. No need to try to do something, or not do something. No need to block thoughts and feelings; nor to indulge frustration about such distractions. No need to worry; to feel guilty and regretful. No need to *fix* this natural process of primordial arising of appearance from its emptiness primordial Buddha "groundless ground", the *Perfect Sphere of Dzogchen*; the perfect imprint/seal of *Mahamudra*.

Buddha told, "Leave it alone; it's perfect as it is". You can't improve it! Connect to that Buddha mind love-wisdom through mindful *shamatha*, and through your stainless, if less than perfect, *bodhicitta* conduct. It will make you happy now. That is the Path.

The Lamas tell that in this nondual view and spontaneous non-meditation practice, all arising unfolding appearance already enfolded in vast unbounded whole that is nondual reality itself is always untainted, undefiled, and perfect just as it is. This basal aboriginal emptiness "groundless ground" is inherently "primordially pure" and uncontaminated by distracting dualistic thought or existence of any kind. The really good news? We now already know this.

Just so, the spacetime forms which arise and exist within and through the formless primordial ground, because there is never a whit of separation from it, is equally inherently perfect just as it appears. Radical teaching indeed. And fortunately, utterly beyond belief. So, it must be *directly* experienced as self-perfected state of *Dzogchen*, now.

Therefore, wonder of wonders, distractions—thinking, feeling, perceiving—negative or positive, are but mere appearances—waves of the primordial natural state upon the vast ocean that is present luminosity of our *undistracted ordinary mind.* There is no *essential* difference! "Form is empty; emptiness is form".

Hence, once again, as Buddha told so long ago, "Rest your weary mind and let it be as it is; all things are perfect exactly as they are". This is the radical nondual View, Meditation, and Practice of the *Dzogchen* path, whether it is introduced at the beginning, or after years of dualistic "development stage" practice. It is this beautiful, simple yet difficult practice that makes it so.

Yes, *undistracted ordinary mind* is simply letting natural mind be as it already is, here now, without adding judgments about distractedness. It's pristine and perfect just as it is, distractions, imperfections and all. That is the radical nondual *Dzogchen* teaching. So we still have to show up for work, take out the trash, and be kind even to "difficult people".

Far from an idealized vacant and void state of mindlessness, undistracted ordinary mind is lucid, awake, vivid, and clear. This again, is nondual, uncontrived, unelaborated *Dzogchen* "non-meditation". As *Dzogchen* founder Garab Dorje told twenty centuries ago, "It is already accomplished from the very beginning", deep within *your* heartmind. It is that profound truth to which we awaken—step by mindful step—upon the mindful mantra breath.

And yes, it takes a bit of peaceful, lucid undistracted mindfulness meditation practice—foundational *shamatha* and mantra prayer, under the guidance of a qualified Lama—to recognize and sustain this state of Presence in the not always so quiescent presence of *samsaric* spacetime reality.

So now, settle into and rest in your familiar state of mindful *shamatha* upon the breath as you receive these kind words of sixteenth century great *Mahamudra* Master Dakpo Tashi Namgyal:

> Look directly into your conscious mind. It is a wakefulness for which no words suffice. It is not a definable entity, but at the same time, it is a self-knowing aware emptiness that is clear, lucid and awake. Sustain this without distraction…Next, examine a particular thought or perception…look into it directly and investigate…No matter what kind of thought occurs, its experience is, in itself, something unidentifiable—it is unobstructedly aware and yet not conceptualizing…As for perceptions, they are a mere impression of unobstructed presence, which is insubstantial and not a clinging to a solid reality. Without distraction then, simply sustain this aware emptiness that is unidentifiable awareness, also referred to as a perceiving emptiness that is perception devoid of a self-nature.
>
> —Namgyal, *Clarifying the Natural State*, 2001, p. 29 ff.

Now, naturally aware mindful Presence and your very own natural mind are one and the same (*samatajnana*). There is no separation. It has always been thus. Open your heart and *feel* that! Then rejoice in this miraculous non-meditation of your *nondual undistracted ordinary mind*! *Emaho*!

What "Undistracted Ordinary Mind" is Not. It is not total quiescence wherein the gross and subtle phenomena of sense perception utterly cease. Nor is it a mindless inert state ("blank Zen") that excludes both sensory input, *and* discursive discriminating wisdom.

It is not a vacant mind state between the arising of thoughts; not empty of sensory experience; not empty of all thinking; not an aversion to perceptual and conceptual experience of any kind.

In short, wonder of wonders, this mildly spooky nondual "non-meditation" meditation of undistracted ordinary mind does not exclude the dualistic experience of ordinary mind! Perceptual and conceptual experience is not the enemy of mindful meditation. Thoughts and feelings, negative or positive, are not the antagonist in this *kosmic* comic play of the mind. And non-thinking is not the goal. Let's not complicate it. Relax a bit and "Let it be exactly as it is". That is the *Dzogchen* non-meditation. Let it be so.

The Witness Presence. So now, just for a moment, place your attention upon your breath, and simply witness your awareness. Be meta-cognitively, reflexively aware of your present awareness; just as it is now. Observe what arises. No need to change it, direct it, evaluate it, think about it, grasp at or reject anything at all. And when grasping/rejecting thinking naturally arises, just witness that. Let it be as it is. Relax and settle into this bright space. Now rest here this moment. Simply feel it. *Feel* the feeling of being you being present here and now. Feel the deep *I Am prana* life current flow of *buddic* Presence of you upon your breath, in this precious moment now.

This primordial Presence cannot be created or fabricated. Why? It is always already present—whether you choose to believe it, or like it, or not. What is, just is. So, feel your connectedness to it, and to all living beings, and to everything that is. That is who *you* are. Rest in That, and be happy now. You are now in good company. All the masters of the three times have told this.

Although the waking state of the untrained mind is brimming with relentless concepts, beliefs and feelings, this undistracted ordinary mind of ours excludes any *distraction* from the "primordial purity" of *bodhi* mind Presence, always present to any and all arising distractions. All embracing primordial wisdom mind Presence is always "primordially present" throughout our myriad distractions. No need to believe this. Let it be as it is.

That direct experience is, Dear Reader, the actual nondual nature of mind; Buddha nature of mind—beyond your concepts and beliefs *about* it. As thoughts and feelings arise, without judgment, return to the bright undistracted state, always upon the mantra breath (*OM AH HUM*), again and again. Or, momentarily shatter a troubling constellation of thoughts/feelings by shouting out *PHAT* to return the mind to its peaceful natural state. "It's perfect just as it is". *That* is human Happiness Itself. Rest a few moments in That! You can think about it later.

Yes, the pristine, undistracted mind state that is liberated from discursive thinking is the moment to moment non-meditative meditation. But a *goal* of utter non-movement of thought, and of perceptual and feeling experience is itself a distraction. As we have seen, seeking a goal of contemplative, meditative happiness as an antidote to suffering is a form of suffering. Wisdom mind/Buddha mind seeks nothing at all. It is complete in itself. And that is who you are. That is the meditation. Thus do we "Make the goal the Path" in this present moment now. Your practice makes it so.

Thus it is, for human beings being here in time, the origin of our discontent is not distracting thoughts and emotions. This is not the real problem. The origin of our suffering is, as Buddha told long ago, primal ignorance (*avidya, marigpa, ajnana, hamartia/sin*) of our always present selfless Buddha nature/Buddha mind.

Thoughts are only thoughts. Emotions are just emotions. They have no inherent power over us that we do not *choose* to give them. So we learn to fine tune our moment to moment choice of where we shall place our attention—on a distraction, or on love-wisdom mind Presence.

Everything is already embraced by clear light undistracted ordinary mind. "Leave it alone and let it be as it is....This cannot be taught" (Gautama the Buddha). So, relax the desire to understand it intellectually. As Lao Tzu told so long ago, "A journey of a thousand miles begins with the first step". Step by mindful step, each moment we arrive.

Thus is the nondual *Dzogchen* View and Meditation the Result/ Fruition of both relative human happiness (*eudaimonia*, human flourishing), and ultimate human happiness (*mahasukkha, paramananda, beatitudo*)—liberation/enlightenment—Happiness Itself. "It is already accomplished from the very beginning". It's too simple to believe; but to present to deny. Please consider well this nondual *Dzogchen* View and Practice.

We have seen that the *goal* of the practice of the spiritual Path is not the yogi's bliss, nor some future perfect nondual happiness mind state; nor is it liberation from suffering. Goals can be future-looking distractions. And the future never shows up! It's too busy becoming the present moment. So surrender your happiness seeking strategies. The goal is simply the practice itself, just as it is now. Abiding in this clear light basic space of vast empty unbounded whole that is the already present all embracing *Perfect Sphere of Dzogchen* is always only here now. It's like coming home.

Thus it is. So be it. May all beings be happy.

No Time, No Self, No Problem

Without past, present, future; empty awake mind.

—Ju Mipham

Neuroscientists and Zen Masters agree: the not so conscious cognitive activity of the human mind is about 90 percent self-centered—I, Me, Mine—and about 90 percent negative: 1) *Aversion;* fear, anxiety, anger, hostility, hatred, guilt, shame and blame; and 2) *Attraction/attachment;* self-ego-I desire, greed, pride—all of it arising from self-centered human "ignorance" (*avidya, marigpa*). Yet even in ignorance, kind gentle Christ-Buddha love-wisdom mind—luminous Presence of That—is always present. How is this so?

Both Jesus and Buddha have told it. Our Wisdom Mind Presence is not a super cool edition of self-ego-I. Yet, our love-wisdom mind primordial Presence transcends yet embraces our self-sense. Alas, as Jesus told, "That which you seek is already present within ... and it is spread upon the face of the world ... but you do not see it." The not seeing it Buddha called ignorance (*avidya, marigpa*). Jesus called it *hamartia*/sin) ignoring our "supreme identity", always already present luminous love-wisdom mind Presence that dwells deep within the human heart and mind. Well, Presence of what?

Because we arise, abide and have never departed the "supreme source" that is our basal primordial emptiness ground of everything that appears (emptiness, dharmakaya, Tao, Brahman) we are necessarily an imprint, an instantiation, an aspect, a face and voice, in a word the Presence of That (tat, sat) vast nondual, trans-conceptual unbounded whole—awareness-consciousness reality being itself—by whatever name or concept.

Self and No-Self Being Here in Time

Intelligent questions like "What is the ultimate nature of self?"; "What is the ultimate nature of *kosmos*?"; "What is Buddhahood"?; "What is the purpose of being human?"; and all other such self-stimulating metaphysical/philosophical questions and conceptual answers are considered by the wise to be ultimately unanswerable dualistic distractions, conceptual fabrications and elaborations. Told the Buddha, metaphysical abstractions do not further human awakening. So, from the relative view, such speculation may quickly become a gilded cage of concepts, beliefs and biases for distracting practitioners from the direct, trans-conceptual love-wisdom Path.

Buddha declined to comment on such questions. Buddha declined to either affirm nor deny the existence of self. Buddha taught only what is fundamental to awakening from the ignorance (*avidya*) that is the root *cause* of suffering. "It is only suffering and its cessation that I teach" (*Anguttara Nikaya*).

Theravada master Ajahn Thanissaro (2015) speaks: "Is it not more fruitful to speak of what one can do, than to speak of what one is"? Yes. Yet in order to speak of what one can do, one is perforce referred to the non-conceptual, contemplative direct experience of *who* one actually is, one's authentic, "supreme identity" as indwelling already present Buddha mind Presence. That is our "supreme source" in whom one's highest capacity arises and expresses itself. It is through this spirit that we most skillfully speak and act for the benefit and happiness of living beings; and through such conduct accomplish our own happiness. After all, we're all in this reality boat together.

Lest we here succumb to the pernicious dualism of a false dichotomy, let it be said that the path of awakening utilizes our *two voices of wisdom*—conceptual understanding and doing, and non-dual contemplative feeling and knowing. We learn to practice these two as a unity.

Ultimate no-self love-wisdom mind Presence—grounded as it is in the vast primordial whole that is formless being itself—empowers and guides relative-conventional self-ego-I in this delightful dance of geometry, always becoming our being here in spacetime form.

That said, discursive concept-mind is not inherently good or bad. Yet, as Hamlet said, "Thinking makes it so". All of the love-wisdom masters of our Primordial Wisdom Tradition have told it, we must skillfully use our conceptual minds, in concert with our moral feeling sense, in choosing what to adopt, and what to avoid; and to intellectually understand what and how (not why) we must establish and continue a trans-conceptual quiescent mindfulness meditation practice, that we may more fully realize just *who* it is that we actually are. We use relative self to awaken to selfless wisdom mind. As Buddha told so long ago, *"No-self is the true refuge of self"*. Relative self and ultimate no-self are a prior ontic and epistemic present unity. No *ultimate* separation. No dilemma; no problem at all.

So, it is the rational mind of relative self-ego-I who *chooses* to practice the ultimate emptiness and compassion of no-self; who chooses to connect to one's selfless indwelling love-wisdom mind Presence. Yes. *Human happiness is a choice.* And so ignorance (*avidya, hamartia*/sin) is a choice. And so the fear/anxiety that sponsors ignorance and its adventitious emotional afflictions—anger, hostility, hatred, ego desire, greed, envy, pride and the rest—is a choice. How is this so?

Both human happiness and human suffering arise from our present *mind state! Thus do we train the wild horse of the mind in moment to moment* placement of attention *upon our quiescent inner peace—bright Presence of That—ultimate human Happiness Itself* (Appendix A).

Time—past, present, future—the perennial "three times" abide in this fleeting *present* moment that is to brief to grasp and hold. This very instant is already becoming the past as it simultaneously receives the future. So this prodigious moment now is *ultimately* illusory. The past is but a *present* memory of what is gone. And the future? It is a present, often fraught anticipation of that which has not yet arisen. So, past, present, and future are ultimately illusory! While time—the three times—are relatively, conventionally (Relative Truth dimension) all too real to an experiencing conscious observer presence, yet from the non-conceptual, nondual ultimate view (Ultimate Truth dimension), time itself is illusory.

Well, what has this time consideration to do with what the Buddha termed the primary human emotional affliction—namely, *fear*? Fear and its subtle cloak that is anticipatory anxiety—from which the other "emotional poisons" (anger, hatred, greed, envy, pride) arise—is not *inherently* existent here and now; though it sure seems so. Fear is present as an anticipation *about* a non-existent event, something that might cause our physical death, or worse. Recall Buddha's teaching on the impermanence (*anitya*) of the relative existence of all conditioned phenomena being here in time. Everything that arises shall decay and pass away. So, fear is excess emotional baggage that we choose to engage, or not to engage. That is the question. How is this so?

We have a *choice* as to where to place our present attention-awareness—upon our fearless love-wisdom Buddha mind Presence—or upon anxiety about the future. Just so, we may choose to indulge regret, guilt, and anger about the past, or not. This amazing choice is cultured through contemplative mind training, in a word, meditation. I have called the development of such mindfulness yoga—*awareness management*. And yes, managing our present attentional awareness requires, like most things noble, assiduous practice, with relief and release arriving in step-functional stages. That is the truth of the matter. Indeed, we should all feel better already!

Be That as it may, real existential danger—atavistic lions, or thieves in the night—are right here and now, undeniably all too real. But the spectrum of fear—from anxiety/worry to panic and terror—is a compelling emotional response to that which does not exist here and now. Fear and anxiety are ubiquitous human emotions. Viewed holistically they are a dark phantom of our imagination, not real or solid at all. Danger is real. *Fear* of a future event is not real.

So, don't believe everything you think. Thoughts come, and they go. Thoughts are just thoughts, empty of substantial real existence. Careful consideration and practice of this truth is the beginning of the fearless liberating wisdom view.

Not much help to a patient at the onset of an uncued anxiety/ panic attack (get them up immediately and walk); or to a student with anxiety or phobic disorder.

Broadly construed, Sigmund Freud attempted a century ago to show that a conceptual, logical, intellectual understanding of one's present neurotic fears and their presumed past causes yields a cure. "Make the unconscious conscious." Sounds reasonable. But it didn't work. The reason is clear. Conceptual knowledge alone, even with emotional cathartic relief, does little to change long term habitual behavior. How shall we understand this?

The *objective*, conceptual cognitive dimension of self-ego-I— human reason with its scientific knowledge—is a wondrous gift. But it must be completed by its counterpart, our inherently *subjective*, trans-conceptual love-wisdom mind—peaceful, loving Presence of That. And that requires contemplative practice, and courage in the face of impermanence (*anitya*), our onto-pathological omnipresent fear of nonexistence, in a word, spooky *death*.

We've seen that our human cognition has two faces, two voices— objective, rational, "scientific"; and subjective, contemplative, spiritual. I have called these "the two faces of wisdom". Obsessively rational Greek materialism—that has now entirely colonized the Western mind and culture—is our prevailing cultural dominate trope, namely, the ideology of Metaphysical Scientific Materialism/ Physicalism. This "scientific" ideology has been agonizingly slow to grasp this urgent noetic doublet—exoteric objective and esoteric subjective—that is the prior unity of human cognitive life. (Please refer to the *Introduction* above for a brief review of the four dimensional structure of human cognition).

Scientific Reductionism. "Science" by its nature is reductive. It naturally reduces matter to smaller and smaller units. For example, the realm of biology, life, is reduced to the principles of chemistry, which reduces its atomic structures to the subatomic particles of physics—quarks and leptons (*Appendix D* "Idols of the Tribe").

Yet, wondrous scientific method has burdened itself with cognitively cumbersome metaphysical baggage known to philosophers of science as "metephysical scientific reductionism"—the unproven and unprovable belief that all phenomenal and cognitive processes are reducible to purely physical brain structure and function. Of course there is no empirical evidence of such a meta (beyond) physical truth. This "functionalist" materialist/physicalist bias is then a non-empirical metaphysical system of belief—to wit, our deep cultural background Greek materialist "global web of belief", Quine (1969).

Our "common sense" objective concept-belief cognition is grounded in this nonobjective system of metaphysical presuppositions. Just so, empirical science is founded in the same uncertain metaphysical principles—Metaphysical Local Realism, Metaphysical Materialism, reductionism, causality, and the rest. Even the foundational axioms of logic and mathematics that produce *deductively* certain conclusions, are uncertain and incomplete, as evidenced by Kurt Gödel's 1931 Incompleteness Theorems, and Werner Heisenberg's 1928 Uncertainty Principle (Boaz "Quantum Logic" 2021a).

But, as Ken Wilber has pointed out, "hidden metaphysics is bad metaphysics". Let us then recognize and acknowledge our discomfiting, but quite natural metaphysical belief biases, lest we fabricate destructive individual and collective ultimate truths of them.

It seems that the *ultimate* nature of *relative* appearing spacetime reality (these Two Truths: emptiness and form) is beyond physics, that is to say the primordial dimension of Ultimate Truth is, *ipso facto,* the realm of post-empirical meta physics. No problem at all—unless we choose to reify and defend such beliefs as absolute truths.

Is our obsessive grail quest for absolute *objective* certainty inherently doomed to failure? Perhaps there are more things in heaven and earth than are dreamt of in our materialist philosophy. This at least is certain: our endless quest for certainty shall have to extend itself into the post-empirical, trans-conceptual subjective realm of our wisdom mind noetic doublet—objective and subjective.

The subject-object unity that is nondual Wisdom Mind tames the objectivist-physicalist bias of the obsessively thinking Western mind, and unifies our objective and subjective human natures. As if these two were ever separate in the first place.

Yes, human being here in ultimately illusory, but not relatively illusory time includes both objective conceptual and subjective trans-conceptual cognitive capacity; both relative self and ultimate no-self. We need them both. The wisdom unity that is Buddhist contemplative *shamatha-vipashyana* meditation practice, with mantra prayer, accomplishes that. Let us then penetrate more deeply into our innate, always present indwelling selfless Buddha mind.

Our Buddha Mind: Self and No-Self

The three pillars of the Buddha's teaching are: 1) *Suffering*, the omnipresent suffering (*dukkha*) of living beings, its cause and cure; 2) *Emptiness/shunyata* of all appearing phenomena as impermanence (*anitya*), selflessness/no-self (*anatman*), and interdependent arising (*pratitya samutpada*); and 3) *Buddha nature*, awakening to the innate Buddha nature/Buddha mind always already present in all beings; then its compassionate expression in human beings as *bodhicitta*—altruistic thought, intention and action to benefit living beings.

The Buddhist Path to liberation from suffering is the assiduous practice, under the guidance of a qualified Lama, Roshi, or Ajahn, of these three foundational pillars, practiced as a unity. Thus do we enter the luminous mind-stream of the Buddha.

The practice of the Path reveals the cause of suffering—primal ignorance (*avidya*) of the impermanence, selflessness, and interdependent arising of all phenomena. These must be understood, and surrendered. Skillful selfless action/*upaya*—compassionate *bodhicitta*—is the primary cause of human happiness. Self-centered, unskillful action under sway of ignorance increases the suffering of beings, and therefore our own cause and effect negative karma—the primary cause of human unhappiness. Told the Buddha, *"What you are is what you have been; what you will be, is what you do now."*

Upaya is the selfless wisdom of our all-embracing Ultimate Truth reality dimension manifesting as skillful compassionate activity in the dimension of spacetime conventional Relative Truth. Recall, these are the Buddha's Two Truths—the Buddhist dominant ontological trope—boundless *shunyata*/emptiness, and spacetime form arising therein. As Buddha told in his lapidary Prajnaparamita *Heart of Wisdom Sutra*: "Form is emptiness; emptiness is form. Form is not other than emptiness; emptiness is not other than form."

Upaya or skillful means/method asks this urgent question: "What actions within my present sphere will cause the most long term benefit to sentient beings in form?" *Upaya* is nothing less than a noetic wisdom imperative that requires, not a final surrender of self-ego-I, but a skillful centrist middle way balance between our relative compassionate ego-self acting in the world for the benefit of beings, and our ultimate no-self love-wisdom Buddha mind that empowers such an ethic of beneficent action. Self and no-self, together at last. As if they were ever separate at all. Yes,*"No-self is the true refuge of self."* Both relative human flourishing and ultimate human happiness/liberation is the result of this union of relative self and ultimate no-self—the Buddha's Two Truths.

We've seen that for beginning bodhisattvas—we Buddhas in training—*upaya* acting in the world through our personality self-ego-I may be understood as an awareness-attention management skill set nurtured and guided by one's own living spiritual mentor. This truth has been taught by all the wisdom masters, *mahasiddha's*, and sages of the three times—past, present, future.

The awakening process to our innate Buddha love-wisdom mind Presence is first the establishment of *shamatha*, "mindfulness of breathing"; then step by step self-ego-I non-attachment to all this seductive impermanent (*anitya*) stuff in the world. This includes attachment to our own blissful mindfulness practice. And it includes fear of death. Our physical death is real. Fear of it is excess psychic baggage. Practice reveals this great truth.

Thus may we envision (*samadhi, satori, vipashyana*) that all experience is *inherently* good—"basic goodness"—because all physical and mental phenomena arise from their pristine, untainted, perfectly subjective boundless emptiness ground—the *Perfect Sphere of Dzogchen,* Great Perfection—the nondual Great Completion of the dualistic wondrous Buddhist Mahayana Causal teaching vehicle.

Once again, Buddha told, "Let it be as it is and rest your weary mind; all things are perfect exactly as they are." In Chinese Taoism this great expression of *Ultimate Truth* (*Tao, Wu*) is known as *Wu-Wei*—selfless, effortless and spontaneous compassionate action for the benefit of sentient beings. Such skillful action arises only from the selfless, pristine purity of the boundless whole, primordial ground itself that manifests for the wise as love-wisdom mind Presence—direct experience of That—by whatever name or concept.

Yet, cautions the Buddha, do not expect the conceptual logical proof of the realm of Relative Truth to "prove" Ultimate Truth: "Do not depend upon logic, inference, analogies, scripture, agreeable views, or probability" (*Kalama Sutra* 3:15). Awakening to selfless no-self/*anatman* wisdom mind Presence is trans-conceptual, non-discursive direct yogic contemplative experience (*yogi pratyaksa*). Wonder of wonders, it is self who *chooses* to practice this supreme happiness no-self teaching. No need to denigrate or deny self-ego-I. No need to fabricate a spiritually way cool Atman "Higher Self". *Let it be as it is.*

Therefore, Buddha's no-self *anatman* need not be an off-putting, pragmatically impossible denial or proscription of self-ego-I being here in relative time, but a call for a skillful centrist middle way liberation strategy, under the guidance of a qualified master, wherein relative self and ultimate no-self work peaceably together in the samsaric dimension of Relative Truth. Enlightened awareness management is the key.

And yet, in the *Dhammapada* we again hear the nondual view of Ultimate Truth: *"Sabbe dhamma anatta"*—"All phenomena are no-self". Ultimately, relative self is surrendered, subsumed and embraced in the selfless, ultimate primordial boundless emptiness ground—no-self itself. Complementary opposites: Suzuki Roshi's Ultimate Big Mind and Relative Small Mind together, always a prior and present unity. How remarkable! Practice makes it so. Let it be so.

Hence, the proper question is not "Who is my true self?" The answer to the atavistic question, "Who am I" is this: "I am that I Am Presence" of the primordial boundless selfless whole in whom this all arises. To borrow an ancient Vedic pith, *Tat Tvam Asi*: That I Am!

Now we understand that our primordial wisdom mind Presence is utterly free of the false dichotomy of self and no-self. Self/form and no self/formless emptiness are the interdependent, dialogical and complementary unity of human being here in time and form. It's worth repeating, "Form is empty; emptiness is form." Here ends the dialog of relative self and ultimate no-self. This selfsame unity "Is already accomplished from the very beginning" (Garab Dorje). No problem at all.

The Metaphysics of No-Self

Gautama Buddha told it well, "No-self is the true refuge of self." Let us remain present to that as we conceptually unpack this splendid kosmic irony that is the notion of *anatman*, or selflessness.

So, let us now engage a bit of *vipashyana*—analytic penetrating insight meditation as a thought experiment.

The *mahasiddhas* and masters of our great Primordial Wisdom Tradition have told it: the *ultimate* nature of this all too real *relative* self-ego-I is a mind-created illusion to which we desperately cling, lest we cease to exist. It seems we are bound by an atavistic onto-pathological terror of nonexistence, which has become the dominant motif of our mortal physically embodied lives, ruled by this unruly, all too real fearsome self-ego-I. Yet, before we were born, no problem at all. An old Zen koan: "Who were you before your parents met?" No self, no fear. No fear, no anger. *Wisdom mind no-self is a peaceful refuge for stressed out self-ego-I—when we remember. No self, no problem.*

Self-ego-I: in its actual true nature it is not a permanent, singular, independent, solid or ultimately real entity. Well, what pray tell is it? Where is it? Who is it? "Hey, it's I-me, this body and mind, right here!" And who is that, other than an empty name and a physical bag of bones with a brain. But where in "I-me" does this mystical self-sense abide?

Self is not findable by neuroscience, nor physics, nor psychology. To paraphrase Leibnitz, if the brain were as big as a mill one could walk in and search for days, but never find a trace of any self-ego-I. Self is nonlocal and non-physical. No physical nor mental location nor local place of any self in brain, nor heart, nor gut, nor anywhere else has ever been discovered. Therefore self-ego-I cannot be body, brain, nor the central nervous system. It is utterly unlocatable and undiscoverable!

Moreover, no entity, no physical nor mental phenomenal structure that controls the presumed self has ever been found. There exists no independent, permanent ego-I that continues through all of our moments of consciousness (the "binding problem" for philosophers of mind). Our sense of self is not a singular independent entity, but a veritable committee of selves. For Buddhists, self is an interdependent continuity of countless previous causes and conditions (dependent arising/*pratitya samutpada*). The self-sense with its desires, thoughts, emotions and judgments is evanescent and impermanent with no purely objective reality at all. Yet, this mysterious apparitional nonentity that we have come to know and love is right here, an all too relatively real phantom—illusory on all accounts—no more real than a series of fleeting thoughts. Self and no-self; strange bedfellows indeed!

This Buddhist view of no-self/*anatman*—the ultimate emptiness of appearing reality and of a permanent observer-independent separate self to perceive it—is shared by modern physics. As Albert

Einstein told, "All of spacetime reality is an illusion, albeit a very persistent one" (Boaz 2021a).

Thus, from the nondual (subject-object unity) *ultimate* view, self-ego-I does not exist! Still, here we are, an all too real *relative* illusion, a mind created proto-religious mystical belief system with not a whit of inherent or ultimate objective existence. Yet it utterly controls our lives! *Kosmic* irony indeed.

The way out of this conceptual conundrum is the way in to trans-conceptual *shamatha*, mindfulness meditation. The *objective* logical syntax of language largely precludes *subjective* knowledge that is *ipso facto* beyond its dimensional reach. This inherent limit of objective conceptual human cognition is only a problem if one insists that the vast boundless whole that is reality itself in whom this all arises is exhausted by mere objective conceptual thinking. Are we not more than that?

How is it that we may come to know this? Thus are we led by time and circumstance to explore hitherto unknown dimensions of our human cognitive awareness-consciousness continuum: to wit, cognitive state 3)—trans-conceptual contemplative, and even state 4), perfectly subjective nondual—as we have seen above.

It is mindful meditative stability that finally establishes an empowering perfectly subjective *certainty* as to the actual illusory nature of self-ego-I, thereby lessening its destructive grip. Ironically, it is this rational "explanatory gap" between the fearsome conceptual uncertainty inherent in self, and the quiescent trans-conceptual reality of no-self Presence, that finally results in nondual noetic (body, mind, spirit unity) certainty.

Some of our wisdom tradition masters have named this paradox the "wisdom of uncertainty"—which is the resolution of the pernicious "paradox of seeking" the happiness that is always already present as our innate, indwelling love-wisdom mind Presence, by whatever name, concept or belief.

Such love-wisdom clarity gradually deconstructs the destructive thinking and activity of narcissistic ego-I. And this requires considerable "ego strength", self-confidence, conceptual intelligence, and yes, courage. It requires a bit of courage to deconstruct this *fantasque* non-entity that we have come to know and love as I-Me-Mine.

Moreover, we are told by the wise that it is an error to make the *goal* of meditation practice the dissolution or destruction or transcendence of the ego-I. Buddha told it well—self and no-self function together as cooperating complementary opposites. A Faustian bargain with the devil? Recall, Buddha's "*Sabbe dhamma anatta.*" All phenomena are no-self/*anatman*. In the subtlest, highest ultimate view no-self love-wisdom mind (*buddhajnana, buddhadhatu*) embraces and guides self, like a loving mother corrects her child. The odious false dichotomy of *either* self *or* no-self is dead. Self and no-self are a prior and present complementary unity. And now we can see it.

But wait! If there is *ultimately* no self, who is it that creates karma in the *relative* world of time and space? Who is it that practices *bodhicitta* conduct for the benefit of non-existent beings? Who is it that acts out all these nonexistent nouns? Who is it that experiences happiness, liberation, enlightenment?

Relatively construed it is self-ego-I. Ultimately viewed it is no-self—our selfless love-wisdom mind Presence of the unborn, unceasing vast boundless formless whole itself in whom this dimension of spacetime form arises and is instantiated. Again, to awaken to our indwelling no-self wisdom Presence we need a healthy, fluent, intelligent sense of self. Ultimate nondual no-self already embraces and subsumes this conceptual duality of self and no-self, well beyond dense "thicket of views" about self and no-self; beyond the skeptical demand of concept bound self-ego-I.

Thus it is, this false dichotomy of self and no-self is fabricated by the infernal machine of obsessively objective human concept mind—unbridled "wild horse of the mind". In the subjective meditative quiescence of trans-conceptual *shamatha/sati*, there is no such problem. Wisdom understands this truth. As 20th century Zen Master Suzuki Roshi told, "No self, no problem."

In such a unitary view, opposing opposites are always dialectically complementary. Light and darkness, existence-nonexistence, life-death, true-false, good-evil, matter-spirit, particle-wave—our dualistic realities require both poles of every dilemma. There is always a plurality of levels of understanding within each pole of a dilemma. Course mind grasps at and defends its singular biased view. The natural holistic cognition of the yogi/yogini's mind sees a greater syncretic truth in the all embracing whole.

Suzuki Roshi on Zen Mind/Wisdom Mind: "In the beginner's mind there are many possibilities; in the expert's mind there are few." The red flag of cognitive bias is, in this regard, an unmistakable feeling of ego defensive affront in the bald face of any kind of challenge to one's well defended personal opinions and belief systems—collectively, our "global web of belief (Quine 1969). To paraphrase Zen Master Hakuin, "A teaching that provokes one's ego defenses is probably a good teaching."

Therefore, let us henceforth view these two conceptual dimensions—relative spacetime form/self, and ultimate formless emptiness/no self—as an ontic prior, yet epistemic present indivisible nondual unity. And when we forget, let the discomfiting red flag of ego bias come to your cognitive rescue.

"Form is empty; emptiness is form." From the metaphysical ontology you choose, arises the phenomenal reality you deserve.

My own cognitive biases being as they are, let us now very briefly revisit the Buddhist view of this curious complementary duality that is relative self and ultimate no-self; our reentry into the Buddhist Mahayana Two Truths dominant trope, namely, Ultimate Truth (*paramartha satya*), formless, trans-conceptual, nondual primordial awareness-consciousness ground, unbounded whole in whom arises the spacetime dimension of Relative Truth (*samvriti satya*), the $E = mc^2$ of physical and mental form.

Self and No-Self: The Buddhist View Revisited

In Mahayana/Vajrayana Buddhism—Sutra, Tantra, and *Dzogchen*—the prevailing view as to the *ultimate* existence of self is this: no-self, non-self, not-self, selflessness, *anatman* in Sanskrit, is the absence or emptiness of an enduring, permanent, continuing singular

Atman-Self, soul-self, "Higher Self". This is the ultimate truth of the "no-nature" of self-ego-I.

This is perhaps the main difference between the *Buddhadharma* and the Hindu *Sanatanadharma* whose view is that ultimate self is a permanent and eternal, reincarnating *Atman* Self that is one with infinite *Nirguna* Brahman, absolute Ultimate Reality itself that transcends but includes, and is the formal and final Creator First Cause of everything that exists. This dualistic theistic Parabrahman ontology parallels theistic God the Primordial Father—*Yahweh* of the Judaic-Christian tradition.

We find the *anatman* no self view well developed in Middle Way *Madhyamaka Prasangika* of Nagarjuna's great 2nd century *Mulamadhyamakakarika;* and as well in the 5th century *Yogachara* School of Vasubandhu. We also find, to the surprise of some scholars, early proto-Mahayana *anatman* in *Dhammapada*, and in other *Pali Canon* texts.

Hence, narcissistic ego-I, our self-sense, is alive and well in the dualistic, objective spacetime cosmic dimension of Relative Truth—the world of Suzuki Roshi's "Small Mind"—even as it is absent and empty of intrinsic existence in the Ultimate Truth *kosmic* dimension that is Roshi's all-embracing "Big Mind".

The *Pali Canon* Hinayana Theravada tradition view of self differs from the Mahayana view of self. Broadly construed, for *Pali Canon*, in this realm of local spacetime Relative Truth, we must not deny or repress or suppress self-ego-I, but wisely and skillfully lift, correct, and work with it. Self and no self must enter a relative dialog and work together toward the ultimate happiness of compassionate enlightenment (*bodhi*), all the while maintaining an acute awareness of ego's subtle duplicity. Self and no-self are already a complementary unity. This was Gautama the Buddha's teaching (Boaz 2020).

Therefore, as we have seen, it is an error to denigrate, deny, or try to transcend the ego-self. After all, it is the anxious ego-I that *chooses* to establish a freeing mindfulness meditation practice in the first place.

Again, in the clear words of the Buddha, *"No-self is the true refuge of self."* No-self love-wisdom mind Presence already embraces the separate self-ego-I. It bears repeating, in the ultimate view, form/self and emptiness/no self are a prior inseparable present unity.

In all the Buddhist canons—*Pali,* Tibetan, Chinese—luminous Presence of no-self—ultimate happiness of That—arises in and through kind, generous, compassionate thought, intention, and action for the benefit of sentient beings. Indeed, on the accord of the masters and *mahasiddhas* of our wisdom traditions such a life style is the very secret and primary cause of human happiness.

Self and No-Self: Review of the View

Self-ego-I is really real in the dimension of Relative Truth (*samvriti satya*), but does not *ultimately* exist in the timeless perfectly subjective dimension of nonlocal nondual Ultimate Truth (*paramartha satya*)—Suzuki Roshi's "Big Mind" that transcends yet embraces the local dualistic spacetime realm of "Small Mind" Relative Truth. Yes, self is relatively really real, yet, as Middle Way *Madhyamaka* Buddhist founder Nagarjuna told, it is "empty of any shred of intrinsic existence".

Self-ego-I is, for Middle Way Vajrayana Buddhists, but a *relative* conceptual imputation, a concept-mind reification and elaboration of an *ultimately* empty illusory non-entity. Such is the Buddha's Two Truths View—Relative and Ultimate—as to the nature of *atman*/self. Yet, this self-fabricated "I" is all too real in the relative conventional world.

Contemplative practice reveals the true nature of self as nonconceptual "innate intrinsic awareness" of indwelling *buddic* Presence, our luminous innermost love-wisdom mind itself. Self arises from, and is always embraced in That. So, while relatively unruly and narcissistic, ultimately self has never departed the vast Buddha mind in whom it arises. Please consider this teaching of the Buddha when feeling down about yourself, or others. Recall this wisdom truth touchstone: *"Let it be as it is and rest your weary mind.*

All things are perfect exactly as they are." That is the ultimate truth of the matter, after all.

Essence of self is then selfless fearless no-self wisdom. This self-less wisdom Deep guides self-ego-I to choose, continue, and complete the practice of the Path—all the way to the end of it. Wisdom mind Presence is always a *choice* of physically embodied ego-I, until relative ego self and ultimate no-self are recognized, then realized as a noetic nondual unity. Or so we are told by the subtlest trans-conceptual nondual teaching of the masters of the Mahayana, the Vajrayana, Theravada *Pali Conon*, and indeed of most of our Great Wisdom Tradition (Boaz 2020a).

The practice of the path recognizes, then realizes that this consciousness processional of the *relative* spacetime and the *ultimate* transcendent dimensions that are the ageless Two Truths of reality are now and forever a prior and present complementary unity, indivisible, inseparable, like a golden thread of the invariant *one truth* that pervades and traverses the fabric of all that arises and appears from the primordial *dharmakaya* ground—nondual unbounded whole itself (*dharmadhatu*).

I shall here reaffirm that our human cognitive awareness-consciousness continuum of understanding has roughly four dimensions or strata: 1) pre-conceptual ordinary direct perception; 2) exoteric objective, discursive, semiotic conceptual cognition; 3) esoteric, subjective, contemplative, mostly non-conceptual cognition; and 4) innermost esoteric or "innermost secret" perfectly subjective nondual cognition—direct *yogi pratyaksa*. These four are an always already prior and present unity. The Buddhist, Hindu, or Taoist meditation master experiences this unity, more or less continuously. For the rest of us, "post-empirical" mindfulness *shamatha,* mantra, and deity practice offer glimpses, "brief moments many times" of this luminous fourfold unity.

If this all seems a bit obscure, let us recall that our binding "mind-forged manacles" (William Blake) are cast off through *shamatha* or "mindfulness of breathing". There remains within this peaceful quiescence of the mind a trans-conceptual, numinous innermost awareness Presence that is always present throughout all of the thoughtful machinations of obsessively thinking self-ego-I. Knowing this we may conceptually unpack our love-wisdom mind gifts and integrate them into our always evolving materialist cultural "global web of belief" (Quine 1969)—perhaps with some cognitive and emotional growth. It is here that self and no-self begin their fruitful dialog on the path to a happy reunion.

Being In Time: How Real is It?

Philosophers, physicists, and Middle Way Buddhists agree, being here in time requires the *relative* presence of a spacetime existing conscious observer-experiencer self. Absent such a conscious self-presence, who is it that could witness and verify a local real existing spacetime? Just who is it that is being here in time? An observing self is *relatively*, conventionally required. But must this self be *ultimately* existent? Theoretical physicists and Middle Way Buddhists say no. How shall we understand this?

The view of reality that holds phenomenal appearance to be ultimately real/existent is known as Greek Representative Realism; in the West it is Metaphysical Local Scientific Realism, ontic handmaid of the prevailing cultural metaphysic that is Metaphysical Scientific Materialism/Physicalism. Such ontic views of the ultimate nature of reality—whether realist or idealist—are "metaphysical" because they admit of no physical, scientific, empirical, observer-independent proof. Such reality statements are rather, observer-dependent. Their logical status is necessarily that of an opinion, or of a metaphysical (literally beyond physical) presupposition.

Ironically, the semiotic/linguistic conceptual structure of the human mind precludes deductive logical proofs of its own existence! For absolute certainty we shall have to leave our state/stage 1) and 2) cognitive dimensional comfort zones and penetrate state/stage 3) and 4). A "leap in fear and trembling", to be sure. This requires a bit of emotional and cognitive courage. We have plenty of cognitive biases to discourage such a scary leap.

That appearing *relative* spacetime reality was *ultimately* illusory was the view of Einstein, Bohr, Heisenberg, and Schrödinger; and it is the view of recent relativistic quantum physics and cosmology, which unwittingly point to the great Buddhist truth of the *ultimately* illusory nature of an all too *relatively* real objective self-ego-I, abiding in a spacetime objectively "real world out there" (RWOT). Einstein told it well, "Spacetime is an illusion; albeit a very persistent one". Said the Buddha, "Form is empty; emptiness is form."

This cognitive state/stage 3) and 4) trans-conceptual, even nondual timeless dimension of Buddhist emptiness/*shunyata* transcends, embraces, and subsumes our global materialist/physicalist web of concept and belief—our cognitively confining, not so comfortable comfort zones brimming with all this objective material and mental stuff that bestows upon us a really RWOT, and a self to experience it. Is our beloved RWOT really "empty of intrinsic existence", as Buddha told?

Let us probe a qbit more deeply into the cognitive protocols of our much valorized 20th century physics and cosmology knowledge paradigm.

Local General Relativity Theory, nonlocal (not limited to the velocity of a light signal) Quantum Field Theory, and nonlocal, nondual Mahayana Middle Way Buddhist emptiness (*shunyata*), Taoism (*Tao-chia*), and Hindu *Advaita Vedanta* ontologies (ontology is concern with what *ultimately* exists; epistemology is how we know it) all tell us that appearing time and space arising as $E=mc^2$—even though *relatively*, conventionally "real"— are *ultimately* but a timeless illusion (*avidya maya*).

For recent physics matter/mass is the relative existence of particle-fields participating in the ultimate "vast implicate order of the unbroken whole" (physicist David Bohm). Middle Way Madhyamaka Buddhists call it *dharmadhatu*, or even *dharmakaya*.

For recent physics local particles and their diaphanous nonobjective nonlocal fields are *ipso facto* inherently insubstantial and immaterial. Neither relativistic physics, nor quantum physics, nor Buddhist ontology can find any ultimately, absolutely existing, objectively real physical or mental foundation for such embodied being in time. (Boaz 2021a Ch. VII, excerpted at davidpaulboaz.org)

We have now seen that such a complementary view as to what exists, and how it exists, is known to Mahayana Madhyamaka Middle Way Buddhists as the "Two Truths"—objective, conventional spacetime Relative Truth, and perfectly subjective selfless, nondual (trans-conceptual) Ultimate Truth in which, or in whom this all arises, abides and passes away (Boaz 2020a). This perennial ontology pervades our great Primordial Wisdom Tradition, including recent physics and cosmology.

We have seen that post-Standard Model physics and cosmology (ΛCDM), and much of our premodern Wisdom Tradition— Mahayana Buddhism, *Advaita Vedanta, Tao-chia*—denies a permanent absolute or ultimately existing spacetime reality, including the existence of an *ultimately existing* independent self-ego-I, though in the dimension of spacetime Relative Truth, this self in time is all too real—that is to say relatively, observer-dependently real, but not observer-independently, ultimately real.

In this perennial nondual view human being located in spacetime is *"ontologically relative"*, dependent upon the presence of a cognizant embodied observer-self which then imputes, reifies, names, and designates its own relative-conventional reality. Not exactly a permanent, solid, ultimately existing "real world out there" (RWOT).

The really good news? This *fantasque* apparitional self is already utterly pervaded with the selfless, luminous, numinous primordial imprint or aspect, or Presence of the ineffable boundless whole in whom it arises and participates. "As above, so below", as ancient mystical Hermetic Kabbalah/Christian wisdom tells. Ultimately, there is not an iota of separation, although to the suffering separate self it sure seems so.

Thus it is, self and no-self are always a prior yet present indivisible unity. Again, as Buddha told, "No-self is the true refuge self"— selfless all-embracing primordial ground itself. How shall we know this great truth? Contemplative meditation practice makes it so. It is this love-wisdom mind Presence, by so many names, to which we awaken through the assiduous practice of the Path. That is human Happiness Itself, always right here now. As Buddha told, "Leave it alone and let it be as it is … .This cannot be told in words."

Moreover, our goal is not happiness in some enlightened future mind state. For the wise the goal is the practice of the Path itself, each moment here and now. We cannot *become* happy in the future. But we can *be* happy now! Past and future are elsewhere. Happiness happens only now. The present moment now is when everything happens. As great gravitational physicist John Wheeler told, "Our notion of time (past, present, future) is how we keep everything from happening at once."

Well then, what *is* ultimately real for we honored guests of the relative phenomenal world? In this nondual fruitional view heady ideas of self and no-self are not the real. Soteriological (salvation, liberation) concepts and beliefs *about* future enlightenment miss the point of wisdom Presence now. Only the quiescent mindful breath; non-conceptual feeling-knowing *direct* yogic experience (*yogi patyaksa*) of our now present "supreme identity"—bright Presence of That—is finally and ultimately really real. In awakening to this aboriginal truth it furthers our human conceptual cognition to radically surrender itself to this atavistic theme. As Jesus told, "The rest shall be added unto you".

The Neuroscience of No-Self

I, Me, Mine! We've seen that for both neuroscience and Mahayana Middle Way Madhyamaka Buddhist metaphysics the perceived self-ego-I is nonlocal; it cannot be located anywhere in the brain, nor anywhere outside the brain. It exists only as an adventitious concept! So, self is intrinsically absent and empty of any solid, permanent absolute or ultimate existence. But, may I say it again, ego-I is all too real in the dimensional realm of relative everyday existence—our *fantasque* being here in time. Indeed, the narcissistic destructive self is often construed by thinking folks as a big problem for our species' continued tenure upon this pretty little planet. Let us then penetrate a bit more deeply into the neuroscience and metaphysics of this diaphanous self being here in spacetime (*Ch.1*, "The Neuroscience of Meditation").

Remembering the Buddhist Mahayana Madhyamaka Prasangika Middle Way Two Truths trope, self-ego-I is absent in the nondual reality dimension of Ultimate Truth, but abundantly present in the dualistic world of Relative Truth. Well, *who is it* that experiences all this stuff? It sure *feels* real. How shall we understand this perceptual and conceptual incongruity?

From an evolutionary perspective, patterns of our prodigious self-sense have permitted *Homo sapiens* to survive long enough to pass on our genes, and become our earth's "dominate species" (not that other species will agree with such an impudent presumption). Thus does self-ego-I still arise under certain conditions: 1) existential threats (avoidance), perceived or otherwise; 2) opportunities for desired stuff (approach) essential or otherwise; and 3) desired relationships with other human beings (attraction), or 4) hostile relationships (aversion).

The two defining characteristics of self-ego-I are then, desire *(attraction, greed, pride) and* aversion *(fear, anger, hostility, hatred). This is the Middle Way Buddhist View of self-ego-I.*

This mixed bag of qualities permit us to eat, procreate, and make war. To be sure, these evolutionary patterns possess their respective "neural correlates" in physical brain. But such neuronal activity demonstrates no unique privileged pattern, quality or location relative to other neural processes (the "binding problem"). Prior to the arising of the self-ego-I in one of our above defining conditions there exists no experiential or neuroscientific evidence of its existence, as we have seen above in our rather spooky thought experiment. But within a half second of a perceived threat or insult, or strong desire—*voila*, here is ego-I in all of its narcissistic urgency. In this way do attraction/attachment and aversion/hostility give birth to an adventitious, otherwise non-existent self-ego-I existing in an all too real RWOT.

Thus is this non-entity I call myself—I, me, mine—in the non-dual ultimate view, an illusory phantom. Perhaps we take it too seriously. Perhaps there is a bit of self-correcting humor extant in the entire absurd endeavor that is self-ego-I. The cognitive stress of this absurd human predicament may, I hope, be lightened by a bit of self-effacing humor. Cultivate it your "self". It's wisely delightful!

Thus again, for both neuroscience and Buddhism, self-ego-I is utterly absent and empty of any intrinsic, essential, ultimate, logical or scientific objective existence. And for Mahayana/Vajrayana Buddhists, neither does the ostensible objective reality that the self desires or avoids possess "any shred of *intrinsic* existence", as second century Buddhist master Nagarjuna told. Yet, here it is, in all of its vainglory. So, *who is it* after all that denies or affirms all of this appearing urgent self-existence? Who is it that knows?

No Time, No Self: $E = mc^2 = \Psi$, But Who Is It That Knows?

Buddhists of all stripes, and relativistic physicists agree: there exists in spacetime nor in mythtime, no substantial, observer-independent self. Well then, just who is it that experiences this empty absence of a self in either an illusory relativistic objective spacetime; or in the perfectly subjective space of *dharmadhatu*? Who is it that feels the subtle bliss of our always present, utterly selfless love-wisdom mind Presence? Please consider this wisdom koan:

Who is it that desires to know and to be happy?
Who is it that is afraid and angry?
Who is it that is born suffers and dies?
Who is it that shines through the mind and abides at the heart of all beings already liberated and fully awake?
—David Paul Boaz Dechen Wangdu

Western relativistic physics simply declines to address its metaphysical assumption of this absurd absence of an objective observer-self in an illusory dualistic spacetime reality; let alone any trans-conceptual subjective love-wisdom Presence that embraces it.

For Einstein, time is but a "persistent illusion". No explanation other than this was ever offered by the great physics master, nor for that matter, by recent instrumentalist, antirealist relativistic quantum physics, who paradoxically, requires an objective observer-self to observe the results of its measurements. The physics operationalist rejoinder to such metaphysical questions may be summed up thusly: "Don't ask impudent questions; just do the calculations."

Recent modern science conspicuously avoids metaphysics, even its own hidden metaphysical presumptions and cognitive biases, to wit, the following unproven and unprovable but still unquestionable "scientific" principles of: 1) Physicalism; 2) Objectivism; 3) Material Substance Monism; 4) Reductionism; 5) Local Universal Causal Determinism; 6) The Closure Principle; 7) Methodological Universalism. (*Appendix D* "Idols of the Tribe: The Metaphysics of Modern Science")

Given our human propensity to cognitive bias, and Science's "taboo of subjectivity", perhaps it's better to allow questions that can't be answered, than to allow answers that can't be questioned.

However, for the pioneers of non-objective quantum mechanics—Planck, Bohr, Heisenberg, Schrödinger, and even Planck's pal Einstein—building upon the broad objectivist shoulders of Sir Isaac Newton and his classical relativistic mechanics, objective time does not exist absolutely or ultimately prior to the "collapse" into real time of Schrödinger's subjective quantum wave function (Ψ) by a sentient observer executing a measurement in Einstein's quasi-real objective time (t). At that instant of "wave function collapse", no one can explain how, an objective spacetime reality—an objective "real world out there" (RWOT)—is almost magically bestowed upon we sentient observers. Inherently vexing "post empirical", post-Standard Model "scientific" metaphysics indeed.

Thus, quite ironically does natively random *subjective* Relativistic Quantum Field Theory (QFT, QED) require an *objective* time and the consciousness of a physically "real" observer-self in order to perform its objective quantum measurements. That's physic's common *relative* view. Yet, *ultimately* considered, physic's objective *observer-independent* self, existing in a putative real time (t) is a quantum entangled "nonlocal" illusion.

Observer-dependent "ontological relativity" takes a more nuanced view. Here we fabricate, impute, then reify our objective realities via our cognitive state/stage 2) conceptual "global web of belief" (Quine 1969). Indeed, this is the Buddhist Middle Way Madhyamaka view and practice. (Boaz 2020a, *The Teaching of the Buddha: Being Happy Now*)

Well, what is the existential status of this quantum ideal observer? If it be a human observer, is he or she objective and local, or subjective and nonlocal atemporal? Middle Way Buddhists will argue that it is both, depending on the view—relative or ultimate. Self and its appearing realities arising from the nondual formless primordial "groundless ground" is ontologically relatively, conventionally existent, yet absent and empty any intrinsic absolute or ultimate existence.

This noetic doublet avoids the philosophical problems of both absolute nonexistence of nihilistic Metaphysical Idealism, and absolute existence of the eternalist substantialism of Metaphysical Realism/Materialism. Is this local-nonlocal existence distinction a false dichotomy? Can spacetime stuff like trees and people and stars exist relatively, yet not exist ultimately? Does this forest of stuff *ultimately* exist when there is no observer present to observe it? We have seen that both the Buddha and Einstein thought not. Yet matter continues to appear to our senses. We shall soon see that some deductive logical systems permit such a paradoxical state of both being and not being in time.

Clearly, 21st century nonlocal, nonobjective quantum theory has some unfinished logical and ontological business to attend to before it may presume to embrace and subsume Einstein's General Relativity Theory. (Boaz 2021a)

Has this illusive quantum observer-self epistemological "problem" presented a logical contradiction that contributes to the inherently vexed theoretical incommensurability of the Quantum Field

Theory (QED) and the General Relativity Theory (GRT) formalisms? Indeed it has.

Quantum theory must now begin to explore non-classical, post-Aristotelian alternative formal paraconsistent, three-valued (TVL), or multi-valued (MVL) logical systems which eschew our limiting "truth functional", two valued, true-false, either-or bivalent Aristotelian logic, permitting truth values beyond mere true and false, existence and nonexistence. Indeed, there is a lot of reality between true and false. Such deductive MVL logical systems allow for a proposition to have a consistent truth value that is *both* true and false—just like our everyday reality. The five valued Indian Nyaya logical system is a case in point. The Buddhist Mahayana Middle Way Madhyamaka Two Truths—relative and ultimate—is such a case in point.

Recent quantum logic has attempted to accomplish such a multi-valued logic, with limited success. The prodigious proto-subjective quantum theory has encaged itself in the classical truth-functional 26 centuries old logic of Greek polymath Aristotle.

For an exploration of quantum logic and other MVL systems including the Hindu *Nyaya* five valued logical system, and Buddhist Nargarjuna's Tetralemma see Boaz 2021b, excerpted at "Quantum Logic", davidpaulboaz.org.

Therefore, a prodigious logical/mathematical and metaphysical healing is required to accomplish the great physics desideratum that is a unifying Quantum Gravity Theory (QGT)—the unification of hitherto incommensurable QED and GRT. The continued absence of a consistent QGT has utterly stalled the program of 21st century physics and cosmology. What to do?

Super-Symmetric-Super String-M Theory? Loop Quantum Gravity? Alas, no purely objective theory works! Until the quantum folks get their metaphysical house in order and produce a settled quantum ontology, grounded in a paraconsistent quantum logic, and a *Dzogchen*-like panpsychic/*kosmopsychic* view of ultimate reality, a quantized gravity theory is but a pipe dream (*Appendix C*).

What *is* clear is that not even a QGT can produce an objectively certain metaphysical ontology. The propositions of science and philosophy are, *ipso facto*, provisional, fallible, and objectively uncertain (the "wisdom of uncertainty), always awaiting that next more inclusive, ever incomplete theory. We shall need a bit of spooky esoteric subjectivity to unify our two seemingly incommensurable cognitive paradigms—objective and subjective. Of course, this requires a relaxing of our cultural "scientific" metaphysical "global web of belief" (Quine 1969).

Perhaps physicists and Middle Way Buddhist scholar-practitioners should dialog over pizza and ale, and engage the metaphysics of a "real" nonlocal, observer-no-self presence arising and being here in time; which shall surely illumine the utter mystery of Wheeler's "great smoky dragon"—wondrous gravity—creator and destroyer of worlds.

Is there a correct metaphysical view-belief as to the ontological reality status of an embodied, observing self-ego-I perceiving its appearances? We've seen that there are three ontological options on offer: 1) that an observer-presence is absolutely existent (Metaphysical Materialism/Physicalism); 2) absolutely non-existent (Metaphysical Idealism); or 3) relatively existent but ultimately non-existent (the Buddhist centrist ontologically relative Middle Way)? Quite naturally, such metaphysical questions admit of no purely objective certainty. We require both voices of our innate cognitive noetic doublet—objective and subjective.

What is *clear is that our being here in time requires cognizant presence of a sentient consciousness, by whatever name, who experiences something. No experiencing presence; no experience of stuff. Because we do indeed experience appearances of something, this fact adds rational ballast to a centrist Middle Way view.*

As to such a self being here in a dubious spacetime—what saith our Primordial Wisdom Tradition? We are perennially told by the wise that this physically embodied self, illusory or otherwise, that we all experience so vividly arises and emerges from—and is not separate from—our continuous trans-conceptual "supreme identity", our nondual wisdom mind ground—by whatever name or form (*namarupa*)—selfless, timeless, already present Presence of That. And That is an instantiation of the great primordial unbounded whole itself (*dharmadhatu, shunyata, dharmakaya,* Samantabhadra, Brahman, Shiva, Tao)—the very source and nature of mind.

It is That (*tathata, satchitananda*) *buddic* nondual awareness-consciousness ground, by whatever name or concept, in whom arises all of this embodied beingness participating in quasi-illusory relative space and time; whether or not we, as egos, understand it conceptually, or even believe it. Or so it is told by the wise of the nondual Great Wisdom Tradition of our species.

Here again arises the Mahayana Buddhist Two Truths trope—relative reality arising within the ontologically prior ultimate "supreme source", primordial "groundless ground" itself. Recall, these two reality dimensions are a prior and present one truth *unity, invariant throughout the entire consciousness processional of human cognitive experience—1) pre-conceptual direct perception; 2) exoteric, objective, conceptual, physical; 3) esoteric, subjective, emotional, contemplative; and 4) perfectly subjective, "innermost secret" nondual.*

This vast boundless whole necessarily, mereologically (part-whole relations) embraces its instantiated parts—trees, stars, and all of us. And these interconnected parts necessarily, interdependently participate in that vast whole primordial ground itself in an ontologically prior and phenomenally present unity. *Tat Tvam Asi*—That Thou Art!

Mahayana Buddhists call this continuous arising of stuff "interdependent arising", or "interbeing" (*pratitya samutpada*)—the emergence of *relative* spacetime form from its formless nondual awareness-consciousness emptiness/*shunyata* base (*gzhi rigpa*), a vast causal matrix of prior causes and conditions. As Buddha told,

"Form is empty; emptiness is form". Thus do we receive, experience, and "practice these two as a unity."

On the account of this mythopoetic "logic of the non-conceptual", wonder of wonders, we are never separate from that great whole! We arise, participate and have never departed that vast, unborn, unceasing, unbroken whole. *Voila!* A mereological logical proof for the existence of non-theistic, non-creator, nondual Godhead!

Be that as it may, this trans-rational, trans-conceptual explanation is not at all satisfying to our dualistic conceptual sociocultural "global web of belief", our collective self-ego-I, steeped as it is in its prevailing Greek Metaphysical Modern zeitgeist that is Scientific Materialism/Physicalism. And yes, this Scientific Local Realism metaphysic has now almost entirely colonized the Western mind.

Again, we transcend the inherent cognitive bias of such concept-belief systems via transpersonal mindful breathing practice, quite beyond the realm of mere concept and belief. This is how we connect to our already present no-self love-wisdom mind—numinous Presence of That. Here the conceptual mantra is *"No self, no problem"*, or "Self and no-self are a unity", or "No-self is the true refuge of self"—an essential nondual truth of the wisdom Path that demands a bit of conceptual elaboration, as we have just seen.

Following this imperfect continuity of trans-conceptual quiescent wisdom mind no-self experience, arising self-ego-I then bemuses itself by conceptually unpacking the whole shebang so that this prior unity of the two dimensions of reality—1) relative, objective, physical, and 2) ultimately subjective, emotional, spiritual—might fit our procrustean "common sense" notions (Bertrand Russell's "metaphysics of the stone age") of a purely physical space-time reality with a solid, objectively real embodied self hanging out in permanent "real world out there" (RWOT). And so it goes—for concept-mind.

The immediate antidote and enduring resolution to such ego-I duplicity is relative self surrender to ultimate wisdom of no-self, that they may work together as a wisdom team. This contemplative dialog is the engagement of post-*shamatha vipashyana*—analytic insight meditation. *We have seen that such a result requires a healthy, secure, flexible, intelligent, courageous and contemplatively trained self-ego-I.*

Our iconic, one-dimensional materialist common sense self is rarely so intelligent. Ego-I is disinclined to recognize, let alone realize trans-conceptual no-self. How so? Self, under sway of popular scientific mass culture denies its spooky ultimate wisdom mind dimension by habitually, conceptually reducing it to the mere gross physical dimension, namely, relative monistic physical brain structure and function. This untidy bit of "functionalist" metaphysical conjuring is known to the philosophy of science trade as "scientific reductionism". So, science is inherently unable to answer our relentless question—"Who is it that knows"?

The task of science is to use its ever incomplete theories as conceptual instruments (Instrumentalism) for making predictions about the physical and mental world of our being here in spacetime; not to speculate about the ultimate nature of that world—as Scientific Realism/Materialism does. *Science tells us what matter does, not what matter is.*

Thus, viewed objectively and relatively, the *ultimate* questions still remain. What is the ultimate nature of mind and the mind stuff arising herein? In whom does this all arise? Who am I in relation to That? How do I connect to That? Who is this ultimate no-self posing as a relative self in illusory space and time? Relative objective conceptual answers are clearly deficient in addressing such ultimate questions. Thus do the wise embrace trans-conceptual, direct yogic experience (*yogi pratyaksa*).

The Hindu tradition bespeaks the great truth: *Tat Tvam Asi!*—That Thou Art; That I Am! Jesus answered the question by invoking Moses and the Prophets: "I Am That I Am". What is the ontic, phenomenological, even soteriological status of this prodigious I Am Presence? *Who is it that knows* this numinous indwelling Presence that I Am? Let us then penetrate more deeply into the very *buddic* nature of mind.

No-Self Help: Who Is It That I Am?

From the view of our innate wisdom mind consciousness—*I Am That I Am*, "innermost secret" love-wisdom Presence, vast boundless whole that is our Heart's desire—that which we constantly seek, whether we know it or not. It is That (*tat, sat*) "supreme identity" to which we aspire; That to which we awaken each moment; each mindful breath. Spooky indeed to self-ego-I's concept-mind, and to our deep cultural background (mostly unconscious) objectivist/materialist/physicalist "global web of belief". Indeed, there are more things in heaven and earth than are dreamt of in our conceptual materialist philosophy.

The good news? Self-ego-I, in due course, and by grace, and with a bit of luck, ceases to be a deceiver and obstructer to our psycho-emotional-spiritual growth and becomes a self-interested, but non-judgmental ally in this great process of awakening to our love-wisdom mind Presence. So be kind to this strange guest of your phenomenal world that pretends to be only you. Relate to it and love it as the mother loves and gently corrects the prodigal child. Recall that exoteric ego-self cognition and esoteric *bodhi* mind wisdom mind cognition are not ultimately separate. Self and no-self are a unity.

On the nondual view, exoteric/outer and esoteric/inner understanding—our perennial Two Truths, Relative Truth (embodied self in time and space) and Ultimate Truth (timeless unbounded whole in whom this all arises)—are always already a trans-conceptual, nondual, utterly interdependent prior yet always present unity. Our selfless, nondual, healing love-wisdom mind—primordial nature of mind—already knows this great truth. *Who is it that knows? That is the one who knows.*

As to this profound one truth unity of the Two Truths, Buddha told, *"Let it be as it is and rest your weary mind; all things are perfect exactly as they are"*. Such wisdom expresses the selfless all embracing Ultimate Truth dimension—boundless whole itself—our indwelling love-wisdom mind Presence that endlessly embraces the dimension of Relative Truth, including unruly self-ego-I being here in time. This profound but subtle nondual (subject-object unity) teaching rides each mindful breath. We connect to That upon the *prana* wind of the mantra breath. Lama Professor Anne C. Klein Rigzin Drolma (2006) has told it well:

> The unbounded whole is how and what reality is …
> Open awareness (*rigpa*, presence), fully present to
> that state of wholeness is the knowing of it.

We have seen again and again that this freeing state of knowing-feeling wisdom mind Presence is inherently, always already present each moment now, at the numinous spiritual heartmind (*hridyam*) of the human being. All of the masters of the three times—past, present, future—have told it. This is the nondual "fruitional view" that embraces and subsumes the duality of the causal view—cause and effect—be good and practice now in order to accomplish a happy result later, sometimes much later.

The outer, exoteric understanding of our great Primordial Wisdom Tradition is primarily causal. "Practice this now in order to get that later." This view is represented in the Buddhist tradition by the *Pali Canon* of Theravada, and by the Two Truths motif of the Mahayana Causal Vehicle. *Well, does buddhahood have a cause?* Relatively, a big yes. Practice of the Path gradually awakens us to our already present Buddha mind. ("Does Buddhahood Have a Cause?", davidpaulboaz.org)

Is Buddhahood conditional, in the future, if we practice real good, and be kind to animals? We have seen that fortunately, the future remains forever in the future as it continuously becomes the present moment. The future is but a present anticipation. And our past is past; but a present memory. Both future and past are elsewhere. There is only the present moment now. Everything happens now. That's where the real action is. That is where suffering happens. That is where happiness abides. Yet this eternal, timeless present moment now is too brief to grasp. This present moment is already past. So, we have nothing to which we may cling. We surrender our being in time and rest in the timeless *buddic* nature of mind. That's where buddhahood happens. This spooky bit of logic makes our dualistic notions of buddhahood in some ideal future mindstate quite problematic.

We find the resolution of this duality of the cause and effect view of the Causal Vehicle that is the noble Mahayana, and indeed of our monistic panpsychic Great Wisdom Tradition, in the non-dual fruitional teaching of Buddhist *Dzogchen*, Essence *Mahamudra,* and *Saijojo* Zen (*Appendix C*). We find it in the aboriginal Tibetan *Bön* tradition; in the Hindu tradition through monistic Kashmiri Shaivism; Tibetan Nestorian Christianity; and in Adi Shankara's nondual *Advaita Vedanta*. This nondual fruitional view is alive and well in *Zohar* of Jewish mystical *Kabbalah*, and in Christian Kabbalistic Hermetic mysticism.

Here, in timeless, eternally present now, the fruition—the awakened ultimate happiness result, our Buddha nature "is already accomplished from the very beginning". Ultimately, we are always already That! Mindfulness meditation awakens us to that great nondual (subject-object unity) truth—step by mindful step.

Therefore, we cannot *become* buddhas later; but we can *be* buddhas now. Paradoxically, dualistic cause and effect dharma practice makes it so. As Guru Rinpoche Padmasambhava told, "You accomplish ultimate truth only through relative truth. Practice these two as a unity."

Through devoted practice of the nondual view the awakening mind, brimming with mindful mantra prayer, has little space for adventitious afflictive thoughts and emotions. We devote our human cognitive semiotic voices—meaning/semantics, logical syntax, and practical pragmatics—to the View, Meditation, and Practice of the Path. In due course, and by grace, we awaken to the primordial ultimate happiness—Happiness Itself. As *Dzogchen* founder Garab Dorje told, "To remain here without seeking is the meditation … it is already accomplished from the very beginning." Then we smile a bit at our stressful, dualistic seeking strategies. We have always known who it is that knows. *Emaho*! How wonderful!

Review of the View

Thus it is, it is our indwelling present, nondual, non-causal, transpersonal, trans-conceptual love-wisdom mind—luminous Presence of That—to which we awaken, breath by breath through life force subtle *prana* wind (*jnana prana*, Holy Spirit) energy entering in upon each mindful breath. Solid self-ego-I here dissolves into no-self—primordial boundless emptiness itself. As the *Prajnaparamita* (Perfection of Wisdom) mantra reveals: "*Gate gate paragate para samgate bodhi svaha*". "Gone gone beyond, gone utterly beyond; now perfect wisdom".

The beautiful *kosmic* irony and paradox here is that in the fruitional view love-wisdom mind Presence is, as we have so often seen in these pages, always already present. "That which you seek is already present within you … and it is spread upon the face of the world, but you do not see it" (Jesus, Luke 17). Now we can see it.

"Mindfulness of breathing" bestows direct seeing (*vipashyana, samadhi, satori*), direct yogic perception (*yogi pratyaksa*)—prior to concept and belief—of that which we seek always here in this very moment now; recognition, then realization of That. It is from this realization that *bodhicitta*, effortless, spontaneous thought, intention and action for the benefit of living beings manifests, however imperfectly, in this sometimes hellish relative duality of self (*samsara*) in relative spacetime *samsara*.

No-self love-wisdom Presence lifts and heals our difficult human lot. Mindfulness meditation, "mindfulness of breathing" as Buddha called it, is the skillful method that accomplishes this miracle (*Appendix A*: "Let It Be: Basic Mindfulness Meditation").

Self-ego-I lives mainly in the past and the future. This present moment *now* is hard for us. Throw in some self-aggrandizing, or regretful past/future fantasy/reverie, and we have a bunch of dysfunctional human minds. As good a definition of "human alienation"—our painful "human condition" as any Unhappiness arising as fear, anger, hatred, despotism, war, and the rest are the inevitable result. We now know the way out of this futile cognitive cage. "No time, no self, no problem." Practice that with gentle kindness toward yourself. Watch as this precious *bodhicitta* spontaneously expresses itself through you for the benefit of other beings— human and otherwise. The subtle energy (*la*) of your practice is the power that makes it so.

We've seen that the truth of the matter is that relative self-ego-I and ultimate no-self wisdom mind Presence are a nondual noetic unity. Relative self and ultimate no-self share a relationship of identity or sameness (*samatajnana*). Through the focused power of "placement of attention" we settle in, then rest mindfully in that peaceful space, upon the *prana* wind of the breath, until this life force *prana* energy arises spontaneously, imperfectly as the thought, intention, and action for the benefit of living beings. We have seen again and again that this altruistic precious *bodhicitta* is the primary cause of human happiness. This is called the "bodhicitta of intention". All of the wisdom masters have taught it. Do we not already know this? Let us then accept full responsibility for it, that it may arise as the beneficent *bodhicitta* of action.

We've also seen that our usual seeking quest strategies for human happiness are based in duplicitous , mindless self, the narcissistic separate self-ego-I and its "I, Me, Mine" effort to acquire much stuff, and to control everything, and to gain power over others. Once again, this narcissistic activity of self is known by the lights of the Buddha's teaching as ignorance (*avidya, ajnana, marigpa*). Delusional ego-I is then the root cause of human suffering; not to mention the suffering of non-human beings. The antidote to such body-mind toxicity? Our always present love-wisdom mind Presence, of course. And how do we accomplish it? Mindfulness meditation practice, under the guidance of the qualified mentor or master, of course. So simple. But not so easy. For most people such wisdom action is a fraught low priority.

The great avatars who came to earth to save us from adventitious ignorance have told it well: Said Jesus, "Forget thy self". Such *kenosis* is the "self-emptying" that the great exemplar accomplished, for all beings, and thus for himself. Islam literally means surrender of self. And Buddha, "There is no permanent self....All *dharmas*/phenomena are *anatman*/no-self....No-self is the true refuge of self".

Still, for the Buddha there is a relative conditional self to whom such phenomena continue to arise. So, we tread a skillful middle way between self and no-self. No-self cannot show up for work, nor buy groceries, nor manage the kids. And who is it that chooses to establish a meaningful spiritual practice? Is it not this problematic self-ego-I? For most folks, and even for highly skilled yogis and yoginis, the self-sense is not going to vanish into a puff of primordially pure fairy dust. And if it did, *who is it* then that is happy and liberated? Once again, self and no-self are both in this reality boat together.

Therefore, we imbue this course grasping contrivance that appears here in an illusory time as narcissistic self-ego-I with all embracing great love of our always present selfless love-wisdom mind Presence—like the mother's love that so gently corrects the selfish narcissism of the child.

Please recall, *love* as selfless compassionate action, and *wisdom* as selfless deep understanding are the two limbs of the Buddha's teaching for us.

We "let it be" thus, imperfectly, more or less moment to moment, between endless distractions, upon each mindful breath, and with each mantra prayer, and with each bit of dualistic practice liturgy. It is self-ego-I that seeks and motivates liberation from suffering— Happiness Itself—that is, most ironically, "already present from the very beginning" as our very essential wisdom mind Presence.

In the first few years upon this difficult and joyous Path we need a self-ego-I. No need to deny, transcend, or denigrate yourself; but don't pretend that you can bargain with it for the control over you and others that it desires. Make self-ego-I your ally. Your innate love-wisdom mind Presence is its constant companion and inner guide.

Your outer Lama, or Roshi, or Ajahn, or Rishi mirrors to you that love-wisdom Presence of the "supreme source" that you always already are—your "supreme identity".

Who is it that I am? That I Am! Bright indwelling Presence of That—without a single exception. Know now that "It is already accomplished from the very beginning." Verily, it is this great awakening that is awakening now within you and me upon each mindful breath, and in each mantra prayer, and in each act of generosity and kindness toward a living being. Thus do we "keep the view", even when we forget. And yes, it takes a bit of practiced patience, and a bunch of courage. But that's a good thing!

Historiographical Note: "Truth Is One"

Neither the Buddha, nor Jesus the Christ, nor Mohammed the Prophet, nor Adi Shankara, nor Lao Tzu created a religion. The schools, sects, and cults of organized religion are dualistic human inventions—interpretations of our nondual (subject-object unity) primordial wisdom (*jnana, yeshe, gnosis*), and bear the limits, distortions, and dichotomies of secondary human gross and subtle ignorance (*avidya, marigpa, ajnana*) as we conceptually and experientially unpack their view and contemplative teachings.

That the greater esoteric "innermost secret" nondual, monistic teaching of *Dzogchen Ati Yoga*—The Great Perfection—is historically associated with Buddhism (it arose with its Buddhist founder Garab Dorje, d. 55 CE) does not mean that this teaching began with, or is limited to historical Buddhism (*Appendix B*).

For example, *Ati Dzogchen* was practiced by the ancient pre-Buddhist *Bönpos* of the indigenous Tibetan *Bön* wisdom teaching tradition; and as well by the prehistoric "Twelve Teachers of *Dzogchen*", centuries before the incarnation of the historical *nirmanakaya* Gautama Shakyamuni Buddha (Norbu 1999).

Just so, Saint Augustine told that the great esoteric mystical teaching of Christianity has its antecedents in prehistory:

That which is called the Christian religion existed among the ancients, and never did not exist, from the beginning of the human race until Christ came in the flesh.

Neither does the historical fact that 8th century CE Buddhist Nyingma school monistic nondual *Dzogchen* teaching was influenced by nondual monistic *Kashmiri Shaivism*, Nestorian Christianity, and by nondual *Ch'an*, nor that Chinese *Ch'an* and Japanese Zen were influenced by Taoism (*Tao-chia*) mean that *Ati Dzogchen* is derived from, or reducible to any of these great primordial wisdom teachings.

As we begin to recover from our obsessively objective linear cause and effect habit of mind we come to understand that each of the nondual wisdom traditions of our great Primordial Wisdom Tradition have arisen, not one from another in a historical cause and effect linear chain, although these influences exist, but interdependently, as a spontaneous nondual wisdom continuum. This indwelling *buddic* love-wisdom mind Presence (*vidya, rigpa, Christos*) arises always from the formless aboriginal ground or base (*gzhi rigpa*), "supreme source"—Ultimate Truth—of all appearing form—Relative Truth—instantiated and participating therein.

These various traditions of the great wisdom tradition of our species all respond— whether through dualistic doctrine and belief, or through nondual direct yogic experience (*yogi pratyaksa*), or both—to this luminous ultimate primordial awareness-consciousness ground of being itself. Each tradition has its names for both the aboriginal ground itself, and for the numinous innermost indwelling Presence of that ground, abiding always at the human Heart (*hridyam*). "What's in a name? A rose by any name would smell as sweet" (Juliet Capulet).

Contemplative meditation practice—upon the *prana*/spirit wind of mantra breath, and deity practice—is our conscious finite portal opening into that infinite ground equally for all of us, in every tradition—our subjectively certain connection to That. "Truth is one; many are its names" (*Rig Veda*).

Conclusion: Coming Home

Who is it that I am? *Tat Tvam Asi*: That I Am—vast primordial whole of being itself. Who is it that knows? Our always already present indwelling love-wisdom mind—bright, numinous Presence of That is the one who knows. Therefore, "Let it be as it is and rest your weary mind; all things are perfect, exactly as they are" (Gautama Buddha). Knowing this Ultimate Truth will help you to be happy in the not so perfect world of spacetime Relative Truth. Here then is the Buddhist *Dzogchen* view, expressed by a great 16th century Zen master who had likely never heard of *Dzogchen*:

> From the beginning all beings are Buddha ... When we turn inward and see our true nature, that self is no-self ... our form now being no-form ... our thought now being no-thought ... this earth where we stand is the pure lotus land, and this very body the body of Buddha.
>
> —Hakuin Zenji

"No time, no self, no problem at all" (Suzuki Roshi).

Should you enjoy your awakening to this perfect, loving peaceful Presence of your "innate intrinsic awareness Buddha wisdom mind", already now present within you—if you have not already done so—enhance it by finding a teacher/guide who can introduce you to a qualified living *Dzogchen* master, and a community of like-minded folks to share it with. The benefit to you, and others in your sphere—especially those you love most—is immeasurable.

All of the love-wisdom masters of the great Primordial Wisdom Tradition of humankind have told it: our human realities being here in time—past, present, future—are only this present spacious, timeless I Am Presence—always already right here now at the human spiritual Heart (*hridyam*). Indeed, that is our "supreme identity", without a single exception. Clearly, this great truth far exceeds our human conceptual mind—our "global web of belief". We have seen in these pages how it is that we may understand and enjoy it.

So rest now in indwelling primordial wisdom mind Presence of that "groundless ground"—*Perfect Sphere of Dzogchen*—vast boundless whole of everything arising within it. Yes, that is who we actually are. *Feel* this continuity of awareness Presence more or less moment to moment through "placement of attention"—your present awareness—upon your mindful mantra breath (*Appendix A*). Then *be* the change you wish see.

"When we understand there is no problem whatsoever in this world." It's like coming home. Now you know the truth of the matter. Please practice it. Now arise and do some good. It will make you happy and free.

Thus it is. So be it. May all beings be happy.

Appendix A: Let It Be: Basic Mindfulness Meditation

Enjoy the space between your thoughts.

Happiness Arises From Your Present Mind State!

So, *train your mind* in happiness: peace, free of the habitual thinking of self-ego-I with its unhappy fear, anger, and pride. Meditation is after all a conscious finite portal into infinite peace—spacious, boundless primordial whole of everything arising therein—bright love-wisdom Presence of That, always already present within you *now*. Train your mind in *placement of awareness/attention* upon that aspect or imprint, or Presence of you, in this present moment now. "Mindfulness of breathing" is the meditation that accomplishes this open secret of human happiness. Below are Ten Steps that could change your life.

It's easier than you think. Begin by sitting in a chair, your back straight, hands in your lap, legs uncrossed, feet flat on the floor. Or sit on a cushion, legs crossed.

1. Thank You

Experience deep thanks for the great gift of your life, just as it is now. Accept yourself—all your positive and negative experience—exactly as you are, here and now. Feel your selfless good will intention to benefit all living beings. This is the primary cause of human happiness!

Lower your gaze so that your neck is straight. Relax jaw, neck, gut. Feel the breath in your belly. Now *place your attention* behind your forehead. Close your eyes, raise your eyebrows. This will produce alpha brain rhythm, the peace response, replacing stressful "fight or flight" beta rhythm. Feel a subtle focused fullness in the forebrain. Let the crown of your head open as light streams in from above and meets the *prana* life-force energy rising upon each breath. *Feel* it pervade your entire body-mind—and deep into the earth.

2. **Attention!**

*Now, gather the "wild horse of the mind" by **placement of attention** on your breath. Be present to your breath as it arises in your belly.* Let your mantra prayer begin. Softly recite *OM AH HUM* (see below). This then is your "alpha mantra breath": 5 seconds in; 7 seconds out through pursed lips (12 seconds). Do it 3 to 9 times (36 to 108 seconds). Let your mantra prayer continue, either consciously, or in the background, day and night.

Each breath feel your busy mind settle into its quiet natural state of wakefulness; your clear light love-wisdom mind Presence—*that aspect of you that is utterly one with the great source of everything—your safe place, beyond all thoughts, concepts, beliefs; free of judgment, fear, anger, guilt, pride; free of self-ego-I. No need to think about it. Open and feel it! Be that stillness. Now say to the busy mind, "Peace, be still". Say to the grasping self, "Peace, I Am".*

Thoughts, questions, feelings naturally arise. Briefly greet them. Negative or positive thinking, planning, wandering, worry/anxiety, anger: label whatever arises "distraction". Then surrender it all on the out-breath. Or let it flow by on vast empty space of the sky, like a bird, leaving no trace. *Again and again return attention to the breath.* After 3-5 minutes open your eyes slightly and breathe normally, mouth closed.

As you settle into, and rest in your selfless *wisdom mind Presence,* your breath will naturally be slow and gentle. Enjoy this feeling of delight within you. Feel your connectedness to everything. No need to create it; or grasp at it. Mindful Presence upon the breath is always already present—your "Supreme Identity". Who Am I? *That I Am!*

3. **In-Breath**

Open to receive luminous purifying "life-force energy", sustainer of all life. It has many names. In the East this energy is *prana* or *ch'i* (spirit/breath). For the West it is *pneuma*/Holy Spirit, the very "breath of life", "bio energy", the subtle face/voice of gross physical light/energy/form ($E=mc^2$) arising from formless, non-conceptual, spacious unbounded whole; vast primordial awareness-consciousness ground itself in whom this all arises. *Breathe*, you are alive! Open and receive. Feel it pervade every space of your body-mind.

4. **Out-Breath**

Release thoughts, feelings, past, future, all self-ego-I grasping. Feel your stability deep in Mother Earth. Whatever arises—thoughts, feelings, doubts, happy or not—release it all on the out-breath. Surrender it all. Witness it all dissolve as you return to your breath, again and again. *Let it be just as it is* in this peaceful luminous sky-like space of the mind.

Please consider this well: Thoughts are only thoughts. They come and they go in dependence upon your present mind state. Thoughts are not a solid reality! You are now learning to choose *your realities by choosing your present mind state. All of the love-wisdom Masters of our great Primordial Wisdom Tradition have taught this great liberating freedom to be happy right here now.*

So, more or less absent thoughts, *feel* your selfless, natural clear-light *Wisdom Mind Presence*—subtle peace, clarity, bliss. From this natural spacious mind state the kind, compassionate *activity* of love spontaneously arises in your mind stream—the very secret and primary cause of human happiness. Place your *attention* on that. Let it be so now.

Thus it is, that deep peace which you desire rides the breath. Remain close to the breath. When distracted by anxiety/anger or self-judgment—simply return to already present Presence upon your breath, again and again. When your mind is filled with light of love-wisdom mind Presence, there is no room for the negative stuff. Practice that and be happy.

5. **Presence**

Here, now, breathe. Open your heart and mind and feel your always present indwelling love-wisdom mind Presence of vast boundless whole in whom this all arises. It's right here! That you are now! Subtle Presence of That may be directly *experienced, prior to thinking, as luminous clear-light mind essence—the very Christ-Buddha nature of mind, beyond any name, concept, or belief.*

Now experience this *prana/spirit* life-energy at the crown of your head. Feel it stream in from above upon each breath. Open your heart to receive. Feel it pervade your entire body-mind. Let it flow downward throughout your head, throat, chest, back, *hara* center in the belly, pelvis; then deep into Mother Earth. Feel your fearless stability in earth.

Let this energy of Presence penetrate any discomfort—that self-contraction from your natural life-energy flow: physical tension and pain, sense desire, grief, doubt, guilt, fear/anxiety, anger/hostility, harsh judgments of self and others. Patient love and wisdom heal fear and anger. Your alpha mantra breath is your touchstone to being That now.

Now experience the emotional lift as any and all presently activated "attachment and aversion" are inundated by Presence of this clear light life energy. *Be* for a moment with whatever arises—attractive or aversive. Then surrender it all on the out-breath. Know now you are free of it. Let this light penetrate and pervade space of your entire emotional and physical body-mind: brain, nervous systems, heart, organs, cells, the very atomic structure of your physical/emotional/spiritual being. Now, rest in this feeling of delight within you.

"Let it be as it is, and rest your weary mind, all things are perfect exactly as they are" (Buddha). "That which you seek … the Kingdom of God … is already present within you … and it is spread upon the face of the world, but you do not see it" (Jesus the Christ).

With each breath *feel* healing life energy Presence fill and overflow into your subtle energy field, this light of you that embraces and pervades your whole body-mind. Awaken to this "basic goodness" that you are, prior to our cultural skeptical "global web of belief". But don't *believe* this. Open, *feel* it. Now self-ego-I is tamed, at peace. Rest fearlessly in That.

6. Wisdom Mind is a Choice

"What you are is what you have been; what you will be is what you do now" (Gautama the Buddha). This bright basic space upon the breath is your natural wakefulness—your primordial love-wisdom mind Presence. *Choose* to be that space/peace, here and now, beyond ego: no past nor future; no attachment nor aversion; no true nor false; no judgment at all—just for this moment. No need to think, try or do anything. *Know that your clear-light mind is already awake, kind and wise. Rest in That, each breath. Let it be as it is; calm and clear.*

Love-wisdom mind *practice* is your Path to liberation from ego-centric ignorance and delusion, root cause of human suffering. Stay with it. Your self-ego-I may resist. Notice the bogus excuses. This *choice* is Happiness Itself: kind *relative* human flourishing that does no harm; and *ultimate* happiness-liberation from suffering; the happiness that cannot be lost.

Thus is human happiness very much an awareness management skill set! Happiness arises, not so much from desirable stuff, but from the choice of your *placement of awareness/attention* upon your breath, in this present moment now! No belief, no leap of faith, no authority but your own is required. Simply settle your mind, open your heart, and be fully present to your alpha mantra breath now. That is your *connection* to peace and happiness already present within you. That is the foundation of your love-wisdom mind practice of the Path.

7. Refuge

Now you know this precious space/peace of your *Christ-Buddha Mind Presence*. Take refuge in it often. Breath by breath purify, pacify, stabilize, beautify your mind; a most courageous act; your most urgent activity. Make mindful breathing a priority, *"brief moments; many times",* all day and all night. Soon it becomes a conscious continuity of awareness. Who am I? Feeling *Presence* of that vast whole—"*Tat Tvam Asi*; That I Am*", without a single exception. You have never been separate from That! Feel That, breath by breath. *That is the View. That is the Teaching. That is the Practice. It's like coming home.*

8. **Compassion Meditation**

By this good generated by each mindful breath make this aspiration for the benefit of all living beings: "*May all beings be free of suffering, and the causes of suffering. May all beings have happiness, and the causes of happiness*". This powerful mantra prayer is as well, your *Compassion Meditation* when practiced for a few minutes. "Come and see" what it does for your present heart-mind state of happiness.

Is not your happiness already linked to the happiness of others? We're all in this reality boat together. Accomplish your own happiness through compassionate thought, intention, and action to benefit other beings. It's called altruism. In the East it's *bodhicitta*. It's the magic metric for a good life. So arise, and do some good. It will make you happy *now*.

9. **Real Practice**

Practice requires patience and courage. Patience is the antidote to anger, which arises from fear. It takes courage to face fear. Practice 20-30 minutes or more upon rising; 10-20 minutes upon retiring; and many "36 seconds of bliss" alpha mantra breaths during the day. Peace is always here, between your thoughts, each mindful breath.

Take refuge in your love-wisdom mind Presence often. Feel it at your heart before sleep; and all night long. Be present while eating, walking, working, loving. Lovingly accept yourself as a mother accepts her child. No blame. Anxious, angry? No time? *Take three OM AH HUM belly breaths right now!* Go ahead and do it now. Your goal is *not* peace and happiness in some ideal future mind state. *Make the practice itself your goal*—each mindful breath. "Mindfulness of breathing is the foundation of all wisdom and happiness" (Buddha).

10. The Five Benefits of Mindfulness Meditation Are Always Already Present

1) Body-Mind relaxation experienced as profound peace, for-giveness, healing.
2) Non-conceptuality: beyond self-ego-I thinking, concept, belief, fear/anger.
3) Clarity: mental and perceptual acuity, luminosity, vividness, wakefulness.
4) Deep appreciation and acceptance of your life, and yourself, just as you are.
5) Wisdom Mind Presence: happiness expressed as kind, com-passionate action.

The Power of Voice

Use ancient mantra prayer *OM AH HUM*, a touchstone, during practice—it's all practice—to instantly connect to and protect your primordial *love wisdom mind* Presence. Let it be always in your aware-ness foreground, or background. Free your mind by reciting daily 108 mantras while walking, or sitting. Get a 108 bead mala.

Good Sleep

Engage your alpha mantra breath for a few minutes as you sit on the side of your bed. Now continue to recite *OM AH HUM* silently, on your back, hands over your heart, or at your side, palms down. Settle into your clear light love-wisdom mind Presence.

Now begin your *full body scan. Feel* the gentle peace of *prana spirit wind* life energy throughout your entire body mind. Your crown center is open. Step by mindful step receive life energy flow from above through your crown and throughout your head; then neck, shoulders, chest, arms and hands; then belly and back, pelvic area, legs and feet.

Relax into the light. Let any obstruction to energy flow—ten-sion, pain, worry, anger—flow away on the out breath, and out through your feet and hands. "Rest your weary mind and let it be as it is". Feel life energy *prana* peace pervade your entire body-mind. Now say quietly, "May all beings be free of suffering and the causes of suffering. May all beings be happy, and have the causes of happiness."

As your breath naturally becomes slow and regular, let mantra prayer arise into your awareness background as you assume your normal sleeping position. Let this spirit breath of yours be your love-wisdom lullaby and goodnight.

OM AH HUM?

These three reality dimensions are one prior and present *unity*. *OM* is formless empty space, primordial ground of all phenomena, vast unbounded whole itself. *AH* is like the sun; selfless clear light awareness—light bridge into form. *HUM* is non-conceptual *love-wisdom mind* Presence of *OM*, always already present now within you; light-form gift naturally expressing itself as skillful loving *bodhicitta*—thought, intention and action to benefit living beings. *Who am I? I Am OM AH HUM*: three gates to happiness—body, voice, mind of all the Buddha's and wisdom masters—your instant connection to That! Feel it purify your cause/effect karma. *The benefit of mindful breathing is immeasurable.*

Now you know the "innermost secret" of human happiness. Please consider it well. If you desire it, then practice it. Now arise and do some good. It will make you happy now.

David Paul Boaz Dechen Wangdu:
coppermount.org; davidpaulboaz.org

Appendix B: A Brief History of the *Dzogchen* Transmission

In Uddiyana (Orgyen) in the second century CE, **Garab Dorje** (d. circa 55 CE), the human founder of the primordial *Dzogchen* teaching, in his *Sambhogakaya* form, having received it directly from primordial *dharmakaya* Adi Buddha Samantabhadra (*Tib.* Kuntazangpo), transmitted the great teaching to his heart son **Manjushrimita** (*The Three Essential Statements* or *The Three Vajra Verses*) who then classified these precious texts (*The Dzogchen Nyingthig*), and then transmitted them to **Jnanasutra, Guru Padsambhava** or Guru Rinpoche (*The Khandro Nyingthig*), **Vimalamitra** (*The Vima Nyingthig*), and then to **Virochana** (*The Cuckoo of the State of Presence or Rig P'ai kyu bhug*).

Vimalamitra and Padmasambhava then carried the teaching from Uddiyana to Tibet in the 8th century CE, at the invitation of Buddhist practitioner **King Trisong Detson.** In the 14th century the entire *Nyingthig corpus* was synthesized and essentialized by Nyingma School luminary **Longchenpa** (Longchen Rabjam 1308-1364) as *The Seven Treasuries (Dzodun)*; *The Trilogy of Finding Comfort and Ease*; *The Trilogy of Natural Freedom*; and *The Three Inner Essences.*

In the 18th century, Nyingma master **Jigme Lingpa** (1730-1798) rediscovered the complete *Dzogchen Nyingthig,* which includes all of the above treasure texts, as a root mind *terma (gong ter)* and condensed its essence as The *Yonten Dzod*, which is now known as The *Longchen Nyingthig.*

In this form the *Dzogchen* teaching was transmitted to the masters of the 19th century ecumenical *Rimé* (unbiased, non-sectarian) movement, the effort to overcome the doctrinal sectarian strife of the various schools that began with the 8th through 11th century confrontation between the *Bön* Tibetan indigenous religion and the introduction of Indian Buddhism to Tibet. These lustrous *Rimé* masters actually supported the early *Bön Dzogchen* teaching. The *Rimé* movement founder was Sakya School Jamyang Khyentze Wangmo. Its primary actors were Jamgon Kongtrul, Patrul Rinpoche, and Nyingma *Dzogchen* master Ju Mipham Rinpoche.

This innermost esoteric *Longchen Nyingthig* is generally considered the authoritative expression of the Nyingma School's great nondual fruitional *Dzogchen* tradition—the Great Perfection or Great Completion (*chen*/great, *dzog*/perfect or complete)—studied and practiced at all levels of the teaching—from foundational *Ngöndro* practice, through *Yeshe Lama* practice, to the *Trekchö* ("cutting through), and finally the *Tögal* ("leaping over") teaching series.

Nyingthig means heart-mind essence. Esoterically, the *Longchen Nyingthig*, the *Heart Essence of the Infinite Expanse*, contains the precious heart essence of the aboriginal primordial *Dzogchen* view and praxis. It contains the innermost secret pith instructions—the *upadesha* (*mengagde*)—and is transmitted from *Dzogchen* Master to prepared disciple directly, non-conceptually, from heart-mind to heart-mind. This "innermost secret" practice of *Dzogchen* is *Ati Yoga*, the highest or subtlest nondual yoga of the Nyingma ten vehicles of Buddhist liberation from suffering, then enlightenment itself.

The "ripe" disciple prepares to receive this sacred nondual Ultimate Truth teaching by completing the *Longchen Nyingthig* Relative Truth foundational practices (*ngöndro*) before entering in the secret pith instruction of the *upadesha*/*mengagde* that includes preparatory *Yeshe Lama*, then the *Trekchö* and finally the *Tögal* teaching cycles.

It is told that the *nirmanakaya* Buddha Garab Dorje initially received the primordial *Dzogchen* teaching, in its entirety, as a direct transmission from the *dharmakaya* Buddha Samantabhadra (*Tib.*

Kuntazangpo), primordial *Adi* Buddha, through the *sambhogakaya* dimension Buddha Vajrasattva (Kagyu's Vajradhara/Dorje Chang) from whom emanates all spacetime historical *nirmanakaya* buddhas. Indeed, it is taught by some *Dzogchen* masters, including 20th century master Tulku Urgyen, that the timeless *Dzogchen* teaching was transmitted to its human founder Garab Dorje by none other than our historical *nirmanakaya* Buddha Gautama Shakyamuni, the twelfth of the twelve great *Dzogchen* masters, in his *sambhogakaya* dimensional form as *sambhogakaya* Buddha Vajrasattva (Tulku Urgyen, 1995).

From a relative, conventional historiographic, doxographic view, early Nyingma *Dzogchen* was formatively influenced primarily by certain Indian Buddhist tantras, but as well by the nondual teachings of *Ch'an*, indigenous Tibetan *Bön*, Tibetan Nestorian Christianity, and Kashmiri Shivaism (Chögyal Namkhi Norbu 1996; John Reynolds 1996; Boaz 2020).

The preceding historiographic evidence is based upon extant texts from the 8th through 10th centuries CE, and from recently discovered texts at Tun Huang, China—the *Rig P'ai khu byug* and the *Bas P'ai rgum chung*. However, according to certain *Dzogchen* tantras the *Dzogchen* linage includes the primordial timeless *Twelve Teachers of Dzogchen* (Dodrupchen Rinpoche, *Tantric Doctrine According to the Nyingmapa School*).

Not all of these twelve buddhas were of the local spacetime human dimension. Some of these stellar prehistoric beings predate even the ancient *Bön Dzogchen* Master Shenrab Miwoche (Tonpa Shenrab Miwo) who transmitted the *Dzogchen* teaching cycles in Olmo Lung Ring (Central Asia) circa 1600 BCE (Reynolds 1996). From there the teaching spread to Orgen (Uddiana)/Zhang Zhung, then to Tibet, then to the rest of the world.

Indeed, the *Grathal gyur tantra*, and other such texts teach that the great nondual primordial *Ati Yoga Dzogchen* teaching, by whatever name or form, has appeared in inhabited star systems throughout the *kosmos* for many *kalpas*, long before the arising of our solar system; and will continue long after its death.

Thus it is, for the Nyingmapa, and many other Buddhist schools, and for non-Buddhists as well, the nonlocal, nondual primordial *Dzogchen* teaching represents the pinnacle of all love-wisdom teaching of the three times—past, present, and future. *Dzogchen* view and praxis is therefore most relevant to the prodigious great wisdom task that is now upon us, the real work of unifying our two seemingly incommensurable knowledge paradigms—objective Science and subjective Spirit/spirituality—as we embark upon our 21st century Noetic Revolution in science, religion and culture. (Boaz 2021b, excerpted at davidpaulboaz.org)

David Paul Boaz Dechen Wangdu:
davidpaulboaz.org; coppermount.org

Appendix C: Primordial Consciousness: *Dzogchen* Panpsychism

> Subject and object are only one. The barrier between them does not exist.
>
> —Werner Heisenberg

Panpsychism

There is now abroad in the world cognosphere a paradigmatic primordial stream of ancient, pre-modern wisdom—both West and East—that continues uninterrupted into Modern and Postmodern Western objectivist scientific metaphysical ontology, and as well, into religious ontology. That Primordial Wisdom Tradition is known in the West as panpsychism.

Panpsychism literally means that the all-pervading ultimate nature of appearing reality is mental, or mind. Panpsychism is a proto-idealist ontology, historically aligned with philosophical Idealism, that the mental dimension of reality—basal primordial consciousness/awareness itself—is the formless fundamental ground, the vast boundless whole in which or in whom physical and mental form arises and participates. Panpsychism offers a viable and venerable ontological alternative to Metaphysical Materialism/Physicalism, and to Cartesian Metaphysical Dualism.

In the East panpsychism begins with the earliest Vedas. In the West we see it first in the foundational 6th and 5th century BCE Greek pre-Socratic philosophers—Thales, Parmenides, and Heraclitus. Panpsychism may be seen as the esoteric wisdom

orientation of the primary wisdom traditions of our species—
Hindu Veda-Vedanta, Buddhism, Taoism, and in the esoteric voice
of Abrahamic Monotheism (*Kabbalah*, Gnostic and Hermetic mystical Christianity, Sufism).

This luminous body of basal primordial wisdom includes
the teaching of the greatest minds and spirits in the history of
our species, to wit: Gautama the Buddha, Nagarjuna, Longchen
Rabjam and the Mahayana/Vajrayana Buddhist *mahasiddhas*, Lao
Tzu, Jesus the Christ and the Christian Holy Saints, Adi Shankara,
Parmenides, Plato, Plotinus, Zeno and his Stoics, Spinoza,
Leibnitz, Hegel, Albert Einstein, Niels Bohr, William James, A.N.
Whitehead, and many more. Good company indeed.

Whence Metaphysics?

Metaphysics, on F. H. Bradley's account, is the "discovery of bad
reasons for what we instinctually know to be true". For Scots radical
empiricist polymath David Hume, any text pretending to address
metaphysical questions should be "committed to the flames, for it
can contain nothing but sophistry and illusion". The British empiricists—Lock, Berkeley, Hume—began this anti-metaphysical bias of
the Western Tradition that is with us still. Immanuel Kant briefly
restored a bit of respect for metaphysical truth, but the early 20th
century advent of the "logical empiricism/positivism" cabal that was
to become the proto-religious prevailing metaphysic of the Western
mind—Scientific Materialism/Physicalism—soon buried it.

Metaphysical questions include the relation of mind to body, the
ultimate nature of physical substance and its relation to the mental
dimension, causation/causality, ontology/being and theistic and
non-theistic nondual God; all inherently metaphysical—beyond
physical/physics exoteric materialist "global web of belief" (Quine
1969). That quantum and gravitational cosmology presume to construct propositions as to the *ultimate nature* of any purely physical
cosmos/universe, it too is metaphysics at the macro level—a monistic, physicalist metaphysic that admits of no logical, mathematical,
or empirical verification or proof.

At the micro level of physical reality quantum physics provides ontological (metaphysical) *opinions* and belief systems as to the ultimate nature of the physical reality ostensibly described by their mathematical equations. For example, is Schrödinger's prodigious wave function Ψ reducible to an objectively "real" physical phenomenon; or is it a subjective trans-physical metaphysical process? Are numbers physically real objects, or emblematic ideal Platonic archetypes? Is all this arising physical and mental reality stuff *ultimately* objectively physical; or some spooky subjective panpsychic process; or as the Buddhist Mahayana Two Truths—Relative and Ultimate—view indicates, a bit of both.

All such views express sub-textual metaphysical ontology, not "scientific" empirical objective fact. Such debates are inherently metaphysical, not scientific debates. Again, the prevailing Western metaphysic is monistic Metaphysical Scientific Materialism/ Physicalism—in short, the ultimate nature of all this arising reality is purely physical. But surely the world is *ultimately* physical, after we scientifically reduce the mental and spiritual dimensions down to purely physical brain structure and function (metaphysical functionalism). Is such a radical reduction possible? Probable? Surely Physicalism is just a "brute fact" of nature. But is it?

In the spirit of Hume and the British Empiricists twentieth century ideological hostility to metaphysics (literally beyond physics) has continued through the scientific vogues of Logical Positivism/ Logical Empiricism, Quine's Naturalism, Wittgenstein's "ordinary language" philosophy, and the Physicalism of the Modern and Postmodern Scientific Materialism belief system. Again, this materialist/physicalist metaphysic is the prevailing ontic and epistemic ideology that pervades of all of the sciences, even psychology and neuroscience; and it cognitively trickles down to become the metaphysic of mass mind "common sense Realism", Bertrand Russell's "metaphysics of the stone age". Reality is all and only just physical. Love, compassion, intuition, poetry, religion, spirit—all reduced to purely physical brain electrochemistry in the head!

Moreover, this epistemic Scientific Realism and ontic Materialism of proto-religious triumphal Scientific Materialism ("Scientism" in its most religious fundamentalist raiment) has colonized the Western "common mind" of recent mass culture. And mass materialist culture has embraced modern science's hostility toward metaphysics through its valorization and idealization of Scientific Materialism and the so called "scientific method", largely unaware that such a view is itself a purely metaphysical cognitive presumptive presupposition; a biased belief system.

Metaphysical views are *ipso facto* beyond physics and so, in spite of our deep cognitive background Greek materialist web of belief, admit of no "scientific" empirical or logical proof. Ontology (*ontos/* being), the science of the "what" and the "how" of ultimate existence—of being itself—that is metaphysics expressed in metaphysical statements of belief. Socratic irony?

So, ontology, what ultimately exists, and how it exists is, by definition, metaphysical, beyond the colossal conceptual reach of empirical physics. To habitually, obsessively reduce the boundless whole of vast ultimate reality itself to the subject matter of mere physics is an important brand of "category mistake" that has tragically diminished our human being to Lewis Carroll and Alice's "bag of neurons" relegated to the deterministic darkness of a godless entirely physical universe. We have in the West adopted a metaphysical ontology that leaves us out in the cosmic cold. Dreadful metaphysic indeed.

Toward the Noetic Revolution

Now the good news! We have upon us in the post-Postmodern human cognosphere the advent of a new post-quantum, post-empirical Kuhnian scientific revolution! The secular post-European Modern Enlightenment zeitgeist that resulted in reductionist objectivist materialist physics and cosmology has utterly failed to explain, or explain away its many logical paradoxes and empirical anomalies— not the least of which is spooky quantum entanglement/nonlocality.

Here is Thomas Kuhn's process. Progress in "normal science" has resulted through such unanswerable anomalies in a "scientific crisis" and a "paradigm shift" that yields a new "scientific revolution"—a new scientific knowledge paradigm. As the old Modernist Materialist empirical physics paradigm has failed us, hitherto prodigal flaky metaphysics has recently returned as respectable cognition into the domain of academic philosophy, and so of philosophy of physics and cosmology.

Physicists fear philosophy. But the quantum collapse of old paradigm positivist scientific objective certainty (Boaz 2021) has forced dialogue with philosophers of physics and cosmology, and even Buddhist philosophy, that we may at last discover just what it is that Quantum Electrodynamics (QED) and quantum cosmology actually tells us about the quantum nature of reality, and how to interpret its several competing theories. The consummation to be wished is resolution of critical physics anomalies arising through the logical and empirical incommensurability of QED and General Relativity Theory (GRT).

A refreshing renascent proto-spiritual *sub specie aeternitatis* (from the view of eternity) metaphysical vehicle has now entered the ontic fray to contend with proto-religious Metaphysical Scientific Materialism/Physicalism for metaphysical hegemony of the Western mind. That syncretic wisdom vehicle is the union of Western monistic Panpsychism with Eastern monistic Buddhist Panpsychic *Dzogchen*, the Great Completion.

What Panpsychism is Not

Panpsychism is not panthestic and should not be conflated with pantheism (everything is God), nor with panenthism (God is in everything). Panpsychism is a viable alternative to what is now considered by philosophers of mind and philosophers of physics and cosmology to be the failure of pan-materialism—reductionist monistic Physicalism of 20th century science and philosophy—the view that everything is just physical, or is reducible to the functionalist gambit, that is to say, physical brain function (scientific reductionism).

Panpsychism is also a viable alternative to Metaphysical Dualism—Descartes' two separate, somehow coexisting substances, namely the physical and the mental dimensions of being human here in space and time. Panpsychism has also contributed to viable neodualism theories.

Panpsychism is not a brand of theism, and so it entails none of the inherently vexed, age old philosophical theistic conundrums (e.g. the three "proofs" for the existence of God; the Problem of Evil/Suffering, and the rest) that plague theistic belief in an omnipotent, omnipresent, omniscient and perfectly benevolent anthropomorphic Creator God somehow co-existing beside His separate creations in a brutal world of adventitious unnecessary suffering. Evil, both natural and human is problematic indeed for any self-respecting compassionate Creator God.

The perennial concern and relentless debate about the existence of God must first distinguish between such a *theistic,* objective, concept-belief, even physical anthropomorphic Creator God, and a trans-theistic, trans-conceptual, all-inclusive, all-embracing ontic "supreme source" or ground. Such a panpsychic/cosmopsychic, nondual (subject-object unity), noetic (body/mind/spirit) all pervading *Ultimate* (*paramartha satya*) primordial *kosmic* ground state is nothing less than the vast unbounded whole itself in which, or in whom all of our spacetime *Relative* (*samvriti satya*) conditional physical and mental realities arise and participate. No problematic theism here.

In the absence of such a foundational understanding of metaphysical distinctions between our concepts and beliefs *about* theistic Creator God and nondual all inclusive godhead or basal ground, metaphysical interlocutors face an endless cognitive and emotional disconnect. Our primary Primordial Wisdom traditions have names and concepts (*namarupa*) for such a nondual primordial ground, to wit, *Nirguna Brahman/Parabrahman, dharmakaya/shunyata, dharmadhatu/mahabindu,* Tao, *Ein Sof,* and many more. "What's in a name? A rose by any other name would smell as sweet" (Juliet Capulet).

Approaching Dzogchen Panpsychism

Panpsychism may be broadly construed as the *psychophysical* ultimate nature of all the arising and appearing stuff of reality itself, *sub specie aeternitatis,* by exploring and unifying the ancient pre-modern physical and spiritual basic principles of our great primordial wisdom traditions.

Panpsychism is at root trans-physical or metaphysical. It transcends yet embraces both objective physical and subjective perspectival, *ontologically relative* phenomena. In other words, we create then reify our phenomenal and mental realities via our deep background sociocultural "global web of belief".

Panpsychism, in its most cogent non-atomistic, non-micropsychic raiment is the proto-idealist view that an all-inclusive, all-pervading grounding consciousness—a "primary monism" of the vast mental dimension is the fundamental and omnipresent reflexive ultimate nature of all arising phenomenal physical and mental reality—the vast *buddic mind* as it were, of trans-rational, trans-theistic, nondual godhead, unbounded whole of reality itself. In short, all *relative* spacetime physical, mental and spiritual reality form arises from, participates in, and is instantiated through this all-pervading formless nondual *ultimate* primordial awareness-consciousness ground.

That which we seek in this connection is a syncretic, Primordial Panpsychism—*Dzogchen, Mahamudra, Saijojo Zen, Advaita (nondual) Vedanta, Kabbalah, Christian Hermetic wisdom*—that includes the holistic wisdom of both East and West. Panpsychism has facilitated something of a reformation in hitherto materialist/physicalist Western analytic philosophy.

As the theoretical and later empirical evidence of the "spooky" (Einstein's term) metaphysics of subjective quantum entanglement/nonlocality entered academic analytic and continental philosophy, and then philosophy of science—beginning with Niels Bohr's 1928 Principle of Complementarity, and later John Stewart Bell's " Bell's Proof" in 1964—metaphysics emerged from its cognitive closet after a half century of extremist anti-metaphysical Logical Positivist "hidden metaphysics" (Ken Wilber), with its odious "taboo of subjectivity" (Alan Wallace).

This ontological, nonlinear positivist metaphysic—concealed in its linear objectivist empirical cloak—that is proto-religious fundamentalist materialist Scientism, thoroughly controlled the suggestible 20th century scientific and philosophical mind, along with the mass mind of "common sense" Realism and Materialism, grasping at their purely objectivist/physicalist ideological web of belief. To question the idols of orthodox Scientific Materialism was, and indeed, still is scientific heresy.

Here, we must recall that the prevailing scientific ideology that is monistic Scientific Materialism/Physicalism is a metaphysical view, just as is monistic Idealism, that everything is mental and the physical reality dimension is illusory. We've seen that ontology—what exists, Being Itself—is a synonym for metaphysics and, rather counter intuitively, admits of no logical, mathematical or even empirical proof! Cosmic irony indeed. Hegel called this discomfiting situation "the irony of the world". The world exists but we can't prove it!

Sadly, for ontological, theistic and even cosmological ideologists—and you know who you are—any hope for logical, deductive absolute certainty for your favorite metaphysical ontology is now logically *kaput*. Well then, is this all too real world of arising matter and energy—$E=mc^2$—*ultimately* merely physical? Or is it ultimately *avidya maya*—just a metaphysical idealist mental illusion? Or perhaps an idea in the mind of God? Or a nice amalgam of Metaphysical Cartesian dualism, or recent neo-dualism of physical and mental entities or dimensions?

Once again, these are not scientific questions. These are metaphysical questions. Important ones. Some middle way resolution of these ontic conditions obtains. But alas, we can't prove any of it via the linear two-valued deductive reasoning of logic and mathematics; nor can we consistently argue it on empirical grounds. So the indispensible ontic metaphysical conjecture of the philosophy, theology, even the physics and quantum cosmology trades shall go on, and on.

Hence, what we seek through our engagement with Panpsychism is an ontology that does not nihilistically deny the physical dimension, or the mental dimension; one that opens an ontological *middle way* that includes both.

In short, we need a "top down" holistic "primary monism" (Schaffer 2010) that grounds our physical and trans-physical cosmic duality as participating parts or aspects of a mereologically non-essentialist but inclusive, metaphysically ontic ultimate, all embracing, nondual primordial boundless *kosmic* whole (*dharmadhatu, mahabindu*).

Do not our linear conceptual wisdom seeking strategies finally require a subject-object duality collapse or surrender (*Wu Wei: Tao Te Ching, Ch. 48*) into the basic space of our *buddic* wakefulness that is ultimately this timeless formless awareness-consciousness being itself, primordial ground of human consciousness, and of all of this appearing stuff? Such is our nondual (prior subject-object unity), panpsychic knowledge imperative.

> Objects altogether are a whole, yet separate;
> Being Itself altogether, yet apart;
> In harmony, yet dissonant.
> Of objectivity, there is a great whole;
> And through this, all things arise and pass away.
>
> —Heraclitus (author's translation)

That all said, it seems to me that the many extant variations on this theme (e.g. "bottom up", atomistic micropsychism views) that is the new Western analytic panpsychic adventure into the vexing metaphysics of consciousness (Goff 2017; Goff "Panpsychism" entry in *Stanford Encylopedia of Philosophy*, 2017) are missing the mark that is this propitious and providential trans-objective, unitary, monistic/holistic—in a word *kosmic*—nondual view. Twentieth century Western analytic ideological habits of mind—objectivism, physicalism/substance monism, atomism/micropsychism, local causal determinism, and the invidious closure principle (*Appendix D*: "Idols of the Tribe")— now haunt this brave new world of East-West panpsychic exploration. What to do?

Let us begin with an all too brief introduction to a holistic Western panpsychic variant known to the initiates of the panpsychic clan by the cloddish epithet "cosmopsychism", or worse, "priority monistic cosmopsychism".

We shall herein attempt to integrate this promising view with the parallel holistic panpsychic wisdom of the East as it has arisen in the Vedic-Hindu *Sanatanadharma* through the *Advaita* (nondual) Vedanta of Adi Shankara (8th century), in nondual monistic cosmopsychic Kashmir Shaivism (9th century), and in the 2nd century Two Truths trope of Nagarjuna's Buddhist Middle Way *Madhyamaka Prasangika*, the foundation, on the accord of H.H. The Dalai Lama (2000), of the quintessential *nondual* teaching that is Vajrayana Buddhist *Dzogchen*, the Great Completion of the duality of the Mahayana Causal Vehicle's Two Truths view and praxis.

Dzogchen Panpsychism

I have come to call it such because *Dzogchen* is a panpsychic, noetic (body-mind-spirit unity), *nondual* (not two, not one but trans-rational nondual), *ontologically relative* and perspectival (phenomenal reality is reified, imputed, and designated via our deep cultural background "global web of belief"), therefore non-essentialist (phenomena are absent any *essential* intrinsic or inherent nature), prior and present subject/object unity. This noetic unity abides beyond the odious split of knowing subject and its objects known. *Maha Ati Dzogchen* View, Practice, Conduct and Fruition/Result is holistic, primary monistic, trans-conceptual and nondual. It embraces our primordial wisdom Two Truths (relative and ultimate) trope.

Just so, this *Perfect Sphere of Dzogchen* is all pervading, all subsuming, *ultimate*, fundamental, vast primordial *kosmic* consciousness ground or base (*gzhi rigpa*)—the luminous, trans-conceptual unbounded whole itself (*dharmadhatu*), nondual Spirit Itself, the vast emptiness/openness in which all *relative*, conditional, utterly selfless spacetime physical and mental cosmic phenomenal forms arise, abide and pass away.

Chögyal Namkhai Norbu Rinpoche on *Dzogchen,* the Supreme Source (1999):

The essence of all the Buddhas exists prior to samsara and nirvana…It transcends the four conceptual limits and

is intrinsically pure; this original condition is the uncreated nature of existence that always existed, the ultimate
nature of all phenomena…It is utterly free of the defects
of dualistic thought which is only capable of referring to
an object other than itself…It is the base of primordial
purity…Similar to to space it pervades all beings…The
inseparability of the two truths, absolute and relative is
called 'primordial Buddha'…If at the moment the energy
of the base manifests, one does not consider it something
other than oneself, it self-liberates…Understanding the
essence one finds oneself always in this state…dwelling in
the fourth time, beyond past present and future, the infinite
space of self-perfection…pure dharmakaya, the essence of
the vajra of clear light.

Therefore, this Ultimate Truth of reality itself is generally considered in the Buddhist Mahayana/Vajrayana wisdom vehicle as
Dzogchen (*dzog* means complete or perfect; *chen* means great). Its
nondual contemplative practice is *Ati Yoga.*
Dzogchen arises as the trans-conceptual, non-atomistic, non-
reductionist supreme teaching whose View is shared with what
contemporary students of panpsychism term *holistic primary monistic
cosmopsychism,* a long epithet for a long luminous history of nondual primordial wisdom that arises at the pinnacle of each of our
primary wisdom traditions—the Hindu *Sanatanadharma* as Advaita
Vedanta; the Buddhadharma as *Dzogchen and Essence Mahamudra*;
Taoism as *Tao chia*, Abrahamic Monotheism in which arises nondual mystical *Zohar/Kabbalah*, and Hermetic mystical Christianity.
Of these illustrious holistic panpsychic cosmopsychism variants
the subtlest or "highest" nondual teaching is perhaps *Dzogchen* View
and Practice (*Ch. 3 above*). How is this so? Western philosophical
cosmopsychism—ancient or recent—is not inherently nondual: 1)
it retains tenuous conceptual artifacts and subtle proto-physicalist
cognitive biases; 2) the requisite nondual contemplative grounding
practice or yoga (union, *religio, yogi pratyaksa*), under the guidance

of a qualified meditation master is usually absent. Such a "grounding relation" via trans-conceptual meditative contemplative practice is required in order to transcend these heady dualistic conceptual trappings and actually establish and ground a relative conventional pragmatic, selfless, kind, compassionate practice into the lifeworld moral and political conduct of human beings. A dualistic conceptual, intellectual metaphysical grounding relation without its concomitant grounding in a non-conceptual contemplative practice, and more or less selfless ethical conduct is woefully incomplete.

Thus is the conceptually inscrutable selfless nondual buddic "Wisdom Mind" of our primordial formless "groundless ground"—all pervading awareness-consciousness itself—grounded in psychophysical spacetime form $(E = mc^2)$ as beneficent human love-wisdom conduct. With no such grounding relation in trans-conceptual contemplative meditation practice with its conscious altruistic ethical conduct—thought, intention and action for the benefit of living beings—this Wisdom Mind poetry of the selfless nondual primordial wisdom ground, while very beautiful to the ear, is little more than prosaic, conceptual philosophical self-stimulation.

Sooner or later there comes a point in the relative time incarnation of personal self-ego-I that this self surrenders itself to all-embracing selfless no-self (*anatman*)—love-wisdom mind Presence of That (*tat, sat*)—by whatever name or form. Here, no-self becomes the refuge of self. Thus does self take refuge—almost moment to moment—in that fearless perfectly subjective mind state of primordial no-self, Buddha nature of mind. And that changes everything!

As Buddha told so long ago, "Let it be as it is and rest your weary mind, all things are perfect exactly as they are". No need to suffer the slings and arrows of outrageous self denigration, or compensatory self aggrandizement. No need to try hard to change anything at all. This very subtle understanding of the selfless perennial Ultimate Truth lifts and heals the chaos and fear of Relative Truth self-ego-I being here in relative time and space. Now may we serve the self through the fearless benefit others. And that after all is the very secret of our human happiness; is it not? Let that time come sooner than later. Our personal and collective happiness depend upon it.

Yes, that is the panpsychic "grounding relation" that makes us happy.

In other words, the *relative* conventional *practice* of nondual Primordial Wisdom Mind Path grounds and motivates a more profound *ultimate* understanding of the all subsuming primordial ground itself—our "supreme identity". We utilize the Relative Truth dualistic practice of the kosmopsychic *Dzogchen* path to awaken to nondual Ultimate Truth that is our always already present love-wisdom mind—the very *buddic* nature of mind. Bright Presence of That! This aboriginal ground then arises and expresses itself in the human lifeworld as spontaneous kind, compassionate Conduct—thought, intention and action for the benefit of living beings. In the Buddhist gloss this altruistic process is known as *bodhicitta*.

The Result/Fruition of such a Path is the relative happiness of human flourishing (*eudiamonia, felicitas*), and full *bodhi* liberation/enlightenment that is ultimate Happiness Itself *(mahasuka, para-manda, beatitudo)*, the happiness that cannot be lost.

Profound *Ati Yoga*, the highest or subtlest ninth stage of the nine *yanas* of *Nyingma School's* nondual *Dzogchen* View and Practice provides such a View, Path and Fruition or Realization.

Hence, our intention herein is to complete the best of historical and recent panpsychism, namely holistic primary monistic cosmopsychism in the Great Perfection/GreatCompletion that is kosmopsychic Dzogchen View and Practice. Let philosophers of mind, and everyone else, come to understand this great teaching. The benefit is immeasurable.

Again, our monistic panpsychic/kosmopsychic heirs include such illustrious Wisdom Mind adepts as Gautama Buddha, Adi Shankara, Moses, Parmenides, Plato, Plotinus, Proclus, Spinoza, Leibnitz, Hegel, Royce, Bradley, Fichte, F.C.S. Schiller, William James (dual aspect "neutral monism"), and Albert North Whitehead via his "extensive abstraction" Process Philosophy, whose view that the process order of spacetime reality is the very "concretion" or instantiation of the primordial nature of nondual godhead, for lack of a better name. Heady wine indeed. Ah, the abstruse genius of Whitehead. Not for the metaphysically timorous.

OK, let's unpack this rather spooky nonlocal nondual kosmopsychism a bit.

Cosmopsychism is known to the Western analytic philosophy trade as a viable "top down" holistic, "primary monistic" (the whole is ontologically prior to and greater than its parts) alternative to "bottom up", quasi-physicalist/materialist, atomistic and micropsychic recent incarnations of perennial panpsychism.

In esoteric top down holistic monistic kosmopsychism the cosmic spacetime located atomistic baryonic parts are grounded in the vast nondual unbounded whole itself. On exoteric micropsychic panpsychic accounts the microscopic subatomic purely physical cosmic parts (quarks and leptons) are ontologically prior to the kosmopsychic *kosmic* unbounded whole itself—instead of the other way round.

But the truth of the matter is that mereologically (part-whole relations) the nonlinear nondual boundless whole is not grounded in its participating parts. The whole is greater than the sum of its participating parts. The vast macroscopic boundless primordial whole in which, or in whom this all arises is necessarily ontologically prior to its microphysical parts. The linear atomistic micropsychic explanation is ultimately pluralistic and so views subatomic particle parts as fundamental. This view is a cognitive relic of, and is derived from our waning cultural Western Greek Scientific Materialism/Physicalism ontology.

Primary monist Jon Schaffer (2010) has pointed out that: "Just as the materialists and idealists debate which properties are fundamental, so the monists and pluralists debate which objects are fundamental." Just so, *Dzogchen* kosmopsychic panpsychism is a holistic primary monist, proto-idealist, observer-dependent, ontologically relative, perspectival view that transcends yet embraces dualistic, derivative and reductionist micropsychic views—whether panpsychic or orthodox scientific reductionist.

The entanglement/nonlocality of quantum physics and cosmology, with its requisite observer-dependent "observer consciousness" exoterically parallels such a nondual holistic monistic metaphysical view. David Bohm's implicate order of the vast primordial entangled/interconnected interdependent "unbroken whole" is, as Niels Bohr told, an ultimate "unitarity" whose complementary nonlocal entangled parts participate as the interconnected boundless awareness-consciousness whole itself.

Buddha called such a holistic, monistic ontology "dependent arising" (causally interdependent "interbeing", *pratitya samutpada*), the open empty formless unbounded ultimate primordial consciousness macrokosmic whole itself in which, or in whom this multiplicity of microcosmic relative spacetime form—including all of us—are conscious psychophysical instantiations. Who am I? *Tat Tvam Asi*, That I Am! Without a single exception. We should feel better already.

Panpsychic *Kosmopsychic Dzogchen* Summary

There is much more to be explored in the dualistic *analytics* and nondual, contemplative direct *experience* of the metaphysics of consciousness. I have herein very briefly argued that what I have rather obliquely termed *Dzogchen Holistic Primary Cosmopsychism* (*kosmopsychism*) is a promising and inclusive view as to such a monistic ontic metaphysic. It attempts to address the lingering paradox of materialism in micropsychic panpsychic views through the unification of Western monistic panpsychism with Eastern Buddhist panpsychic or *kosmopsychic Dzogchen* View and Praxis. I have further developed this syncretic metaphysic in a forthcoming book (Boaz 2021b).

The panpsychic monistic cosmopsychism of recent Western panpsychic philosophy of mind (Schaffer 2010), while avoiding some of the realist and materialist scientific reductionism of physicalist atomistic micropsychism, still retains subtle dualistic conceptual traces or cognitive biases of the failed ontology of reductionistic Scientific Materialism/Physicalism. The metaphysical materialist-physicalist bias that matter must be intrinsically only physical substance remains essentially unchanged. No real metaphysical progress here. We require a new holistic metaphysical scientific paradigm that integrates our human *buddic* wisdom mind subjectivity with the prodigious objectivity of the old scientific paradigm. This desideratum devoutly to be wished abides in the new *Noetic Revolution in Matter, Mind and Spirit* (Boaz 2021) that is now upon us.

Here, perceiving subjects and their objects of perception and conception are pre-consciously presumed to be reducible to relative physical substance, observer-independently essentially real stuff with its own *intrinsic nature* in an observer/theory-independent, absolutely objectively "real world out there (RWOT). If this be so, even panpsychic cosmopsychism retains a proto-realist, physicalist, materialist ontological bias, as we have seen.

Thus have I dared to attempt to integrate Western and Eastern metaphysical ontology by introducing Mahayana *Madhyamaka's* foundational *Dzogchen*, the Great Completion/Perfection in a contemporary panpsychic context. Admittedly, this does some cognitive damage to the nondual primordial purity of the *Dzogchen* View.

Mahayana and its causal Middle Way *Madhyamaka Prasangika* is at root a non-essentialist ontology, denying that the spacetime stuff of relative physical and mental reality has any inherently existing *intrinsic ultimate* nature, let alone a purely materialist/physicalist intrinsic nature. Rather, Newton's "furniture of reality" is, for the great nondual Buddhist mind of 2nd century Nagarjuna, utterly selfless, empty and absent "any shred of intrinsic existence". Empty of what? Relatively existing spacetime stuff is empty of any permanent *ultimate* absolute existence (Garfield 1995).

However, mental and physical phenomena are *relatively*, conventionally real by virtue of their appearance in spacetime to a perceiving, designating, reifying consciousness, an often all too real self-ego-I. Still, all this appearing stuff is not *essentially* intrinsically real.

Ultimately, this view of the great whole that is trans-conceptual nondual reality itself describes the reality limit of all appearing physical and mental phenomena—spacetime instantiations of the primordial "groundless ground" itself. This stuff is then relatively, observer-dependently real; but not ultimately, observer-independently real.

Indeed, on the nondual *Dzogchen* view, the spacetime dimension of relative form, arising as $E = mc^2$, has never departed its formless dimensional ground that is all embracing Ultimate Truth. Recall that these two truth dimensions are an inseparable ontologically prior and epistemologically present unity. Nagarjuna told it well: "There is no ultimate difference between (relative) samsara, and (ultimate) nirvana". This is of course the poetic cosmic irony of the duality of the Mahayana Buddhist Two Truths ontic trope that is completed in nondual *Dzogchen*, the Great Completion.

Thus does *Dzogchen*, through its nondual ultimate view, practice, and fruition/realization transcend and complete not only the Two Truths duality of the Mahayana, but as well the implicit, implied or assumed Metaphysical Physicalism and Cartesian Dualism of recent Western panpsychic and cosmopsychic reality accounts of the all embracing implicate unbounded whole (*dharmadhatu, mahabindu*)—noetic (body/mind spirit unity), nondual ultimate reality itself.

Well, what is all that to my own happiness, being here in time? Once again arises the ultimate ontological question: Who am I? *Tat Tvam Asi*; That I Am: luminous, innermost love-wisdom mind Presence of That. This supreme relationship is one of nondual identity—our "supreme identity"—human Happiness Itself.

In *Madhyamaka Prasungika* Buddhist philosophy of mind, this Two Truths View (Relative and Ultimate) represents a Middle Way between the permanent substantival material existence of monistic absolute Metaphysical Materialism/Physicalism so beloved of Western physics and philosophy, and as well, the nihilism of most Eastern and Western monistic absolute Metaphysical Idealism which sees material existence as no more than mental illusory *avidya maya*.

In other words, the great Buddhist *Prasangika* Middle Way acknowledges the reality of the *relative* spacetime dimension of mental and physical *form* or Relative Truth (*samvriti satya*) as it continuously arises from its all-embracing formless ultimate consciousness *emptiness/shunyata* ground (*paramartha satya*), the great all inclusive unbounded whole itself (*dharmadhatu, cittadhatu, dharmakaya, kadag*), the very Buddha nature of mind, and of everything arising and instantiated therein. It is the primordial Presence (*gzhi rigpa*) of our always present Wisdom Mind, our indwelling Buddha Mind (*samatajnana*) that always already knows this great truth.

Again, *Prasangika* denies arising reality any permanent inherent, intrinsic, absolute or *ultimate* existence. This dualistic *Prasangika* Two Truths View is the foundational Mahayana Buddhist philosophy of mind. Once again, its Two Truths ontic and epistemic duality is then completed in panpsychic/kosmopsychic nondual *Dzogchen*, the Great Completion.

Engaging Our Panpsychic Wisdom Mind

While the metaphysics of consciousness has been valiantly and relentlessly reexamined through recent explorations of Western panpsychism—still, our noble analytic philosophers of mind need not reinvent the proverbial perennial panpsychic mindwheel. Consciousness studies and philosophy of mind have been alive and well in our Eastern Wisdom Traditions for at least 35 centuries. Let Western philosophers of consciousness engage this urgent primordial wisdom in the current century.

One wonders how Western philosophy and science has managed to avoid this great nondual wisdom for so long. Are there not more things in primordial consciousness itself than are dreamt of in canonical Western Philosophy and Modern Science? What are we afraid of?

Our pernicious *taboo of subjectivity* has, for the modern scientific mind, veiled and defended Western dualist and materialist analytic philosophy—with its philosophy of physics and cosmology—from a holistic, even nondual metaphysic of consciousness. This is now beginning to lift, due in no small part to our recent revealing cognitive adventures in the proto-Idealism of Western Panpsycism. Perhaps then it's OK to integrate, at long last, the holistic subjective panpsychic wisdom of both East and West with the prodigious objective science and philosophy of the West.

Let Western philosophy of mind and philosophy of science—physics, cosmology, biology and an inchoate neuroscience—now engage nondual Buddhist, Taoist, Vedanta wisdom of the East. "East is East and West is West; and *ever* the twain shall meet". (Apologies to Kipling.)

Now that quantum entanglement/nonlocality, along with Buddhist *Madhyamaka shunyata*/emptiness/boundlessness has utterly collapsed our uncomfortable comfort zone of a purely objective, physical, observer/theory/model-independent "real world out there" (RWOT); and now that the hitherto despotic culture of science and philosophy has granted us its permission to do the transempirical metaphysics of the Quantum, and of panpsychism, let's try something completely different already!

Let philosophers of mind—academic and Buddhist—now engage the exoteric/analytic and esoteric/contemplative exploration of Buddhist *metaphysics of consciousness*. Caveat: this shall require—Yikes!—a bit of spooky Buddhist contemplative practice; that is to say mindfulness meditation, mindful breathing upon our psychophysical spiritual belly buttons.

Or, because meditative-contemplative Presence of the nondual primordial awareness-consciousness whole shebang is "always already" present at the spiritual heart (*hridyam*), and renewed upon the *prana* wind (life-energy, *ch'i, lung, pneuma*/Holy Spirit) with every breath and so cannot be a legitimate future *goal*—mindful, continuous spontaneous *Dzogchen* "undistracted non-meditation" may be the more accurate understanding.

For you see dear Reader, our inherently indwelling, always already present Wisdom Mind, bright Presence of That—by whatever name or concept—if it is to be more than mere intellectual, conceptual self-stimulation requires the compassionate active *engagement* of both facets of our precious noetic cognitive doublet— both objective knowledge and subjective wisdom—a coming to meet as it were of the nondual noetic body/mind/spirit dimensions of our being here as honored guests of the phenomenal world.

Wow! What hath God wrought upon the hitherto psychic safety of comfortable academic philosophy, physics and safe and sane intellectual theistic conjecture and exoteric but powerful petitionary prayer?

Mindful No-Self Help

In any case there's plenty of scientific evidence based medical and psychological metadata to demonstrate that trans-conceptual contemplative mindful breathing practice, by whatever name, expedites human health and well being. And it furthers human evolution toward the conscious discovery and then supraconscious recognition, then "greater esoteric", even nondual liberation/ realization of our otherwise spooky human ultimate identity. This selfless "supreme identity" is our always present love-wisdom mind Presence of That. Is such deep knowing awareness not after all, the function of the wisdom traditions of our species?

Alas, a mind is a terrible thing to mind. Mindfulness practice is blatantly simple; but it's not so easy. Sadly, it requires a bit of self-discipline, and a lot of courage. Yet, there is a veritable Western "mindfulness revolution" now upon us. Check it out for yourself (*Appendix A*).

Please recall here that both human happiness and unhappiness arise from our present mindstate. Minding the "wild horse of the mind"— freeing the narcissistic conscious mind—self-ego-I—from the adventitious afflictive negative emotions (fear/anger/hostility, greed, and pride) seems a very sane approach to *human awareness management.* One might even speculate that the real meaning of outer, inner, and "innermost secret" human body-mind-spirit evolution to be precisely That.

Mindful *Dzogchen Kosmopsychism*: The Grounding Relation

The *Dzogchen* holistic "primary monistic cosmopsychic" or kosmo-psychic panpsychism account seems to me to be one that clearly dodges not only problematic physicalist, emergentist and dualist rejoinders, but as well, the presumed "combination problem"—how is it that panpsychically conscious particle/field micro-subjects combine to constitute the complex consciousness of conscious human macro-subjects—is avoided because human macro-subjects are grounded not in microcosmic particle/field brain micro-subjects—Suzuki Roshi's Small Mind, but in the boundless awareness-consciousness that is the vast primordial whole itself—Big Mind.

As to the vexing and mysterious "grounding relation", the *relative* spacetime microcosm is always already grounded, arises and participates in the *ultimate* holistic primary monistic vast cosmopsychic boundless "implicate order of the whole" (David Bohm)—by whatever name or concept. In contradistinction to "constitutive micropsychism", derived as it is from the materialist metaphysic that everything is grounded in purely physical microcosmic particles and fields, primary monistic cosmopsychism holds that the stuff of reality exists ultimately because it all is grounded in the macrocosmos, the *kosmic* whole of the universe itself (Schaffer 2010).

This then is the essential holistic perennial truth of the subtlest nondual teachings of our Primordial Wisdom Tradition, not the least of which is the all embracing *Perfect Sphere of Dzogchen*, the Great Completion/Perfection.

"Mindfulness of breathing" meditation is the unsurprising, trans-conceptual contemplative methodology for knowing this mereological grounding relationship of ostensibly separate microcosmic parts to their vast nondual macrocosmic whole. Contemplatively merging the wild horse of "conscious mind" with that great quiescent noetic *kosmu* (body mind-spirit) consciousness whole is the method of psycho-spiritual practice that reveals not only the metaphysical understanding of this sublime cosmic process of "the dance of geometry", but the urgent moral depth of human relationships.

This grounding process is not essentially a *physical* merging or combining of micro phenomena with macro subjects. Rather, the deeper, subtler "grounding relation" process is trans-physical and trans-conceptual, albeit with analogous physical "neural correlates" in brain structure and function, always in a context of a connecting morality that is grounded in our epistemic prior monistic cosmopsychic or *kosmopsychic* metaphysical objective-subjective understanding.

The presumption that the grounding relation must be somehow a purely physical process of combining purely physical entities is a discomfiting unconscious ideological relic of our prevailing Western bias that is Metaphysical Materialism/Physicalism. Panpsychism is inherently metaphysics, but as Ken Wilber has pointed out, unconscious physicalist metaphysics is "bad metaphysics". Let our inchoate *kosmopsychic* metaphysic enter the light of a bright new day.

Therefore, in consciousness studies, of which contemplative studies is now a proper participant, the mindfulness meditative panpsychic grounding connection to the trans-conceptual primordial "supreme source"—the very ground of being—is the great process, the Way of our inherent perfectly subjective Wisdom Mind. It changes everything. It's like coming home.

Much has been said by philosophers of mind about the nature of this "grounding relation". Monistic *kosmopsychic Dzogchen* as I have here broadly construed it, employs an acausal/non-causal directly experiential (*yogi pratyaksa*) grounding relation/connection of dualistic *relative* appearing phenomenal reality to/in our nondual *ultimate* basal ontic panpsychic primordial ground itself. And this *gnostic* wisdom process arises in the inherently trans-conceptual, post-rational, post-empirical, even post-metaphysical nondual boundless whole in whom all of our arising and appearing space-time realities are luminous energetic instantiations.

Our nondual, noetic trans-conceptual direct experience of That, upon the breath, may then be conceptually, causally, scientifically unpacked. Our inherent *noetic doublet* is the subjective and objective; inner and outer; physical and mental/spiritual whole. Human cognition includes both at once. These two voices of our human cognition are already a prior and present ontic and epistemic unity. As good a definition of the human condition and its epistemic human predicament as any.

Knowing this—objectively and subjectively (contemplatively) is accomplished through objectively and subjectively engaging intrinsic "open Presence" of our indwelling always already present love-wisdom mind. Sounds a bit spooky? So how shall we do this? As Buddha told, "mindfulness of breathing". It bears repeating. Paradoxically, we use *relative* dualistic objective and subjective practice to fully awaken to our *ultimate* intrinsic wisdom mind Presence of the whole. This then is the prodigious grounding relation of the microcosmic with the macrocosmic dimensions of the boundless whole of reality itself.

The Dzogchen view and practice that is the nondual completion of Mahayana Buddhist Two Truths philosophy bespeaks this dualistic grounding relation as one of nondual identity—the monistic one truth that is invariant throughout all of our human cognitive consciousness processional: 1) pre-conceptual ordinary direct perception; 2) exoteric, objective, conceptual, physical; 3) esoteric, subjective, mental, contemplative, spiritual; and 4) perfectly subjective nondual. These four inherent reality dimensions are not reducible one to the other, as is the case in monistic Physicalism and in monistic Idealism, but represent a complementary ontologically prior indivisible nondual unity. Bold holistic panpsychic cosmopsychic metaphysics indeed.

Approaching the *Dzogchen* Grounding Relation

David Bohm's "implicate unbroken whole" of physical cosmos is subsumed by the even more fundamental, trans-physical, nondual *kosmopsychic Perfect Sphere of Dzogchen*". This all embracing, all pervading immediate awareness Presence (*vidya, rigpa,* I AM) of formless awareness-consciousness itself abides throughout and all about arising cosmic material stuff, these myriad forms that are the contents of the physical, mental, spiritual formless *kosmic* consciousness whole shebang.

Thus does this *relative* dimension of spacetime form continuously arise in/to our human consciousness mindstream from the *ultimate* formless awareness emptiness "groundless ground" that is the great unbounded panpsychic whole (*dharmadhatu, mahabindu*), primordial awareness-consciousness itself—Heidegger's Being Itself; Hegel's nondual Spirit—in whom body and mind are necessarily, luminously already instantiated.

Once again, Hindus and Buddhists speak: *Tat Tvam Asi*. That I Am (That Thou Art). Speaking of this primordial "I AM Presence" of Moses and the Prophets (Isaiah 41:10), Jesus told: "That which you seek is already present within you; and it is spread upon the face of the earth, but you do not see it". And from *Dzogchen* founder Garab Dorje, "It is already accomplished from the very beginning; to remain here without seeking (anything other), that is the Meditation". And Buddha told, "Wonder of wonders, all beings are Buddha". Yet, under sway of Metaphysical Scientific Materialism/Physicalism we miss the mark (ignorance, *hamartia*/sin, *avidya, ajnana, marigpa*)) almost entirely. Our cognitive antidote? Objective philosophical, and subjective contemplative practice. Practice these two as a nondual unity.

As to the "innermost esoteric" perfectly subjective nondual view and practice of our great Primordial Wisdom Tradition—Christian, Hindu, Buddhist, Taoist, Hebrew, Islam—we are taught by these premodern masters and *mahasiddhas* that the numinous I AM Presence of the great all pervading unbounded whole that we are, is always already immediately present in this very moment now. Ultimate happiness, enlightenment, liberation is only ever here now. This present moment now. It cannot be elsewhere. So there is nothing to seek elsewhere. Indeed, everything happens only now.

Therefore, we cannot *become* happy later; but we can *be* happy now. The past is utterly gone beyond, but a present memory. The future is but a present anticipation. So, there is only this present *now.* Yet even this present moment now is to brief to be grasped. It is already future. So, there is nothing solid to which we may cling. There is only this timeless infinite luminosity of the Presence of the "feeling of being". And that's enough. By grace "It is already accomplished from the very beginning". It is that primordial truth to which we awaken through our philosophical (*philo/*love, *sophia/* wisdom unity), and contemplative practice of this prodigious love-wisdom Path.

This then is *Dzogchen* panpsychic/*kosmopsychic* view, practice, conduct and fruition/realization. Thus do we *choose* to train the mind, through the mindful breath, and under the guidance of a qualified *Dzogchen* meditation master in the "placement of atten-tion" upon already present Presence of our "innermost secret" love-wisdom mind. And yes, it requires a bit of simple—but not so easy—unbiased, Zen Mind/Beginner's Mind practice. And that requires a highly intelligent, fluent, holistically oriented, and cou-rageous self-ego-I.

Facing up to the seemingly bad news: with the exception of a few avatars and *mahasiddhas*, sages and saints, we are scarcely awake to our inherent, indwelling always present wakefulness—nondual ultimate consciousness-being itself. Now that's a spooky duality! I have argued that we might well consider the relation of complementarity (Niels Bohr) in our metaphysical spiritual quest for a panpsychic, *kosmopsychic* "grounding relation" between the ultimate consciousness whole, and multiplicity of its participating, instantiating parts—which, by the bye, embraces all of us sentient beings.

Father of the quantum theory Niels Bohr, himself a student of Taoism, would have advised that such a relative-conventional "con-jugate pair" of opposites (subjective yin and objective yang) must be *ultimately* a complementary all inclusive whole—nameless form-less Tao itself. "The Tao that can be named is not the eternal Tao" (Lao Tzu, *Tao de Ching*).

Just so, Tibetan Buddhist luminary and historically identifiable Vajrayana founding father Padmasambhava (8th century) advised:

"The only way to realize the (nondual) wisdom of Ultimate Truth is through (Relative Truth) dualistic practice of the Wisdom Path." Therefore, if you want *this* result, you must practice *that* cause. Relative cause and effect. As Zen Master Suzuki Roshi told: "To know ultimate Big Mind, work with relative Small Mind."

This nondual monistic *Dzogchen* panpsychic *kosmopsychic* view and praxis of ultimate reality itself is a quasi-Schafferian (2010) panpsychic Primary Monism in that it holds not that the whole has no parts, but that the single ontic *ultimate* boundless whole transcends, includes and grounds the *relative* participating parts—indeed, an exemplar of our perennial Two Truths *leitmotif.*

We've seen that the primordial boundless whole itself is fundamentally and ontologically prior to, always already embraces, and is the ontologically *ultimate* trans-conceptual nondual "groundless ground" for all *relative* spacetime arising therein. Conversely, for pluralistic, dualistic atomistic micropsychic panpsychic views the parts are fundamental and are ontologically prior to and ground the whole. The relative epistemic atomistic cart before the ultimate ontic horse of nondual truth?

In other words, this noetic, nondual, nonlocal *kosmic* whole is ontologically prior to, and transcends yet includes the local cosmic spacetime located physical atomic baryonic parts. In this holistic view of ultimate reality the relative, local physical parts supervene (depend) upon and are grounded in the vast primordial nonlocal unbroken whole itself. Just so, the whole supervenes upon the parts. How so? Mereologically, where there are *relative* parts, there is a subsuming, embracing whole. Where there is an *ultimate* whole, there are arising and participating parts. The relative, complementary duality of part-whole are *ultimately* unitary, as Bohr, the Buddhists, and indeed our entire premodern nondual Primordial Wisdom Tradition have told for many centuries.

Yes, in such an ultimate nondual (subject-object identity) view the primary relation of objective parts to the all inclusive perfectly subjective awareness-consciousness whole is one of numerical identity—the two *relata* are one selfsame identity. Relative spacetime human consciousness arises from That (*tat, sat*) ultimate or absolute consciousness whole.

That is the upshot of the objective "grounding relation". The subjective grounding relation is being awake to this great aboriginal nondual truth.

From the dualistic relative-conventional view, a whole and its parts are separate. Thus, this conceptual relative/ultimate duality that pervades and permeates all binary discursive semiotic discourse is reflexively resolved and completed in the *kosmic* nondual all-embracing *Perfect Sphere of Dzogchen*—primary monistic panpsychic *kosmopsychism*, the Great Completion of Buddhist Mahayana/Vajrayana Path (H.H. The Dalai Lama 2000, 2007; Norbu 1999).

We've seen that the peaceful realization of that great truth cannot be a future mindstate *goal*. *Our happiness and our unhappiness are the result of our present mind state. Human happiness happens only now.* Presence of our love-wisdom mind, by whatever concept or belief, is always already present this very moment now. That is the great perennial wisdom teaching. Wondrous paradox to our conceptual "global web of belief" (Quine 1969).

How do we recognize, then realize this truth of human happiness beyond mere concept and belief? We make our *goal*, not happiness, nor liberation, but the practice of the Path itself, upon each mindful conscious breath, again and again—"brief moments many times"—as it becomes, step by mindful step, a radiant continuity of present moment to moment awareness. Zen Master Suzuki Roshi told, "To know Big Mind; work with Small Mind." To personally realize the luminous nondual unbounded panpsychic whole, ultimate trans-conceptual "groundless ground", mindfully engage its primordial consciousness particulars. No dilemma. "No problem at all". As Buddha told so long ago, "Rest your weary mind and let it be as it is; all things are perfect exactly as they are". Awaking to that primordial truth is the real panpsychic grounding relation.

This then is the body-mind-spirit noetic imperative now present in our emerging Noetic Revolution in matter, mind, and spirit.

Appendix D: Idols of the Tribe: The Metaphysics of Modern Science

Toward a post-empirical scientific noetic knowledge imperative

Science and its scientists must make conscious their *a priori* preconscious metaphysical presuppositions, value assumptions and beliefs underlying modern scientific metaphysical ontology, ideology and methodology. These "idols of the tribe" (Francis Bacon) have become the cognitive biases, the "false absolutes" of science that belie the truth of the interdependent unity of subject and object, of experimenter and experiment, of mind and body, of spirit and matter, indeed, of relative/particular and of universal/ultimate reality dimensions.

The biases of "Big Science" have greatly impeded holistic scientific research into the perfectly subjective ultimate base or ground in which appearing phenomena arise—of the nature of mind, of human consciousness and consciousness studies, and of emerging 21st century contemplative studies.

For example, the ontology that the whole of reality is only objective and physical (Metaphysical Realism/Materialism); or that it is only subjective and mental (Metaphysical Idealism) is a qualitative judgment of value, not a quantitative scientific fact. Both of these ontologies are unproven and unprovable metaphysical assumptions. Philosophers of physics and cosmology—if not physicists and cosmologists—are quite aware of this fact, as are Buddhist philosopher-practitioners.

Our much valorized Scientific Materialism (physicalism, objectivism, reductionism) is the "scientific" prevailing ideology of Western culture—the totems of the cult of proto-religious fundamentalist "Scientism". Unfortunately, this concept-belief system still rules the physical, biological and social sciences, the humanities, and indeed, our global mass culture. This quite unscientific religion of science is largely responsible for the catastrophic, narcissistic reduction of our inherent compassionate subjective *spirit,* to mere objective consumable *matter.* Just so, from the metaphysical ontology you choose, arises the phenomenal world you deserve.

Let us now consider a brief summary of these unexamined cognitive biases, assumptions and presuppositions, to wit, the deep cultural background scientific "global web of belief" (Quine) that has now colonized the Modern Western heart and mind.

1. **The Principle of Physicalism (Materialist Realism):** An essentially pre-given separate and independently existing, exclusively *physical* spacetime reality exists as a "real world out there" (RWOT), the basis of all appearing phenomena, *a priori*, independent of observation or experiment by any sentient observer (the "myth of the given"). All appearing reality is absolutely existing *observer-independent* purely physical stuff. Metaphysical materialist/physicalist bias indeed.

2. **The Principle of Objectivism:** This purely physical reality is *ultimately* knowable to *separate* human observers *observer, theory, model-independently* via objective, quantitative scientific observation, experiment and mathematical analysis. Objective empirical proof of this view has remained unfindable for 400 years of European Modernity. The *observer-dependent* phenomena of Middle Way Buddhist view are denied. Here, reality—Newton's absolute space and time—is not just *relatively*, conventionally objectively real (Buddhism), but *ultimately* objectively real (Metaphysical Realism).

On this extremist view, our *subjective* personal and transpersonal experience—love, spirit, God—are not

proper study for empirical *objective* science; thus the pernicious "taboo of subjectivity". Subject and object are irrevoca-
bly split. The noetic, nondual unity of knowing subject and
its objects known—the very foundation of our Great Wisdom
Tradition—is *objectively* unknowable, therefore impossible.
Radical metaphysics indeed.

3. **The Principle of Material Substance Monism:** Material
substance is all there is. There is nothing other than, or
transcendent to, or inclusive of this observer-independent,
purely objective physical reality; no more inclusive whole;
and there is no truth extant, or discoverable, or beyond this
objectivist materialist, realist permanent, eternal substance.
This absolutist substantival view is radically objectively essen-
tialist. No space here for love and spirit.

4. **The Principle of Reductionism:** All subjective experience—private, first person, mental, emotional and spiritual
events and experiences—can be epistemologically *reduced* to
their objective, physical electrochemical neural correlates
in purely objective physical brain matter. Mind, emotional
experience, behavior, love, God are nothing more nor less
than an "emergent property," an "epiphenomenon" or "arti-
fact" of physical brain and its electro-chemical processes. We
are little more than Alice's "bag of neuron's".

Scientific reductionism sees causality is always "upward",
from physical to mental. Holistic "downward causality" via a
primordial consciousness ground, to a mental, then physical
dimension is ideologically denied. On this radically reductionist view, human consciousness is the product of mere
material, physical brain structure and function.

Conversely, in the great wisdom traditions of our species—Veda-Vedanta, Buddhism, Taoism, and the monotheistic traditions—we find that matter, brain and mind arise
from the trans-conceptual, transpersonal formless ultimate
primordial ground, unbounded whole itself, by whatever

name, in which all *relative* spacetime form arises, participates, and is instantiated.

5. **The Principle of Local Universal Causal Determinism:** All events are determined by their local, objective, purely physical causes. If we knew all the initial causal conditions, then we could determine, through classical mechanics alone, with complete certainty all of the effects (objects/events) in the universe (Laplace's Demon). Holistic, "nonlocal" acausal, indeterminate explanation of events is precluded. Here, the metaphysics of modern science with its sacrosanct causal "principal of locality" is at odds with the acausal, nonlocality of its own Quantum Field Theory (QFT) and Quantum Electrodynamics (QED). (Boaz 2021a *The Collapse of Objective Reality: Quantum Nonlocality and Buddhist Emptiness*, excerpted at davidpaulboaz.org)

6. **The Closure Principle:** This purely physical realm of all existence is "causally closed" to any non-objective, non-physical causal or acausal explanation. The validity of any explanation beyond the physical local realist cause and effect dimension is implicitly or explicitly denied. Thus does the incommensurability of relativistic physics with quantum physics arise. The propitious desideratum of a quantum theory of gravity—the unification of the local cosmic with the nonlocal quantum—is *ipso facto* precluded by this naive Closure Principle bias.

7. **The Principle of Universalism:** The preceding "scientific" ideology is the only correct explanation as to the nature of appearing reality, its discovery, prediction, explanation and interpretation. No other views or methodologies can lead to truth. All differing views are in error. Cognitive bias writ large!

Fortunately, a new 21st century global knowledge paradigm—a new wisdom imperative—is now emerging in the human cognosphere. It is nothing less than the post-empirical inchoate Noetic Revolution in science, spirituality, and culture that is now upon us.

(Boaz 2021b *The Noetic Revolution: Toward an Integral Science of Matter, Mind and Spirit*)

Thanks to Werner Heisenberg, Niels Bohr, Willis Harmon, Alan Wallace, Ken Wilber, Jay Garfield, David Finkelstein, Richard Tarnas, Owen Barfield, Amit Goswami, H.H. The Dalai Lama, and the many astute critics of the ideological Physicalism bias that is Modern Metaphysical Scientific Materialism.

David Paul Boaz Dechen Wangdu:
davidpaulboaz.org; coppermount.org

Bibliography

Ajahn Brahm. 2006. *Mindfulness, Bliss, and Beyond.* New York: Wisdom.

Almas, A.H. 2008. *The Unfolding Now.* Boston: Shambala.

Allione, Lama Tsultrim. 2018. *Wisdom Rising.* New York: Simon and Schuster.

Anam, Thubten. 2009. *No Self, No Problem: Awakening to Our True Nature.* Boston: Shambhala.

Begley, Sharon. 2007. *Train Your Mind, Change Your Brain.* New York: Ballantine.

Boaz, David Paul. 2021a. *The Collapse of Objective Reality: Quantum Nonlocality, and Buddhist Emptiness* (forthcoming). San Diego: Waterside.

___. 2021b. *The Noetic Revolution: Toward an Integral Science of Matter, Mind and Spirit* (forthcoming).

___. 2020a. *Mindfulness: 36 Seconds to Bliss.* San Diego: Waterside.

___. 2020b. *The Teaching of The Buddha: Being Happy Now.* San Diego: Waterside.

Bohm, David and Basil Hiley. 1993. *The Undivided Universe.* New York: Routlege and Kagen Paul.

Bohr, Niels. 1934. *Atomic Theory and the Description of Nature.* New York: Cambridge Press.

Carroll, Sean. 2003. *Spacetime and Geometry: An Introduction to General Relativity.* NY: Addison.

Chalmers, David J. 1996. *The Conscious Mind.* New York: Oxford Press.

Chögyam Trungpa. 2015. *Mindfulness in Action.* Boston: Shambhala.

Cozort, Daniel. 1998.*Unique Tenets of the Middle Way*. New York: Wisdom.

Dōgen Zenji. 1986. *Shobogenzo* (trans. Thomas Cleary). Univ. Hawaii Press.

Dowman, Keith. 2010. *Maya Yoga* (Longchenpa's *Gyuma Ngalso*). Kathmandu: Vajra Publications.

Dzogchen Ponlop Rinpoche. 2006. *Penetrating Wisdom*. New York: Snow Lion.

Dudjom Rinpoche. 1991. *The Nyingma School of Tibetan Buddhism*. Boston: Wisdom.

Garfield, Jay. 2015. *Engaging Buddhism: Why It Matters to Philosophy*. New York: Oxford Press.

Gen Lamrimpa; Wallace, Alan. 1992. *Calming the Mind: Tibetan Teachings on Cultivating Meditative Quiescence*. New York: Snow Lion.

Gunaratara, Henepola. 2011. *Mindfulness in Plain English*. Boston: Wisdom.

Gyamptso, Kenpo Tsultrim. 2001. *The Two Truths*. Auckland: Prajna Editions.

Herbert, Nick. 1985. *Quantum Reality*. New York: Anchor.

His Holiness the Dalai Lama. 2007. *Mind in Comfort and Ease*. (Longchen Rabjam's *Finding Comfort and Ease in Meditation on the Great Perfection*). Boston: Wisdom.

_____. 2000. *Dzogchen*. New York: Snow Lion.

_____. 2005. *Essence of the Heart Sutra*. Boston: Wisdom.

_____. 2009. *The Middle Way*. Boston: Wisdom.

Heisenberg, Werner. 1958. *Physics and Philosophy*. New York: Harper.

Hopkins, Jeffrey. *Meditation on Emptiness*. Boston: Wisdom.

Jomgön Kongtrul. 2005. *The Treasury of Knowledge* (Book Six, Part Four). New York: Snow Lion.

Klein; Lama Anne C. 2006. *Unbounded Wholeness: Dzogchen, Bon, and the Logic of the Nonconceptual.* New York: Oxford.

_____. 1998. *Knowledge and Liberation*. New York: Snow Lion.

Lamrimpa, Gen. 1999. *Realizing Emptiness* (trans. B. Alan Wallace). New York: Snow Lion.

Longchen Rabjam. 2007. *Precious Treasury of Philosophical Systems* (trans. Richard Barron). Padma.

_____. 2001. *Precious Treasury of the Basic Space of Phenomena* (Autocommentary): Padma.

Mipham, Jamgon. 2007. *White Lotus.* Padmakara Translation Group. Boston: Shambhala.

Nagarjuna. 1995. *Fundamental Wisdom of the Middle Way* (trans. Jay Garfield). New York: Oxford.

Namgyal, Dakpo Tashi. 2001. *Clarifying the Natural State.* Hong Kong: Rangjung Yeshe.

Newland, Guy. 2008. *Introduction to Emptiness.* New York: Snow Lion.

Norbu, Chögyal Namkhai. 1999. *The Supreme Source.* New York: Snow Lion.

Nyoshul Khenpo. 1995. *Natural Great Perfection* (compiled by Lama Surya Das). New York: Snow Lion.

Penrose, Roger. 2004, 2007. *The Road To Reality: A Complete Guide to the Laws of the Universe.* Vintage.

Pettit, John, W. 1999. *Mipham's Beacon of Certainty.* Boston: Wisdom.

Porges, Stephen. 2014. *Polyvegal Theory.* New York: Norton.

Quine, Willard Van Orman. 1969. *Ontological Relativity and Other Essays.* New York: Columbia.

Reynolds, John M. 1996. *The Golden Letters.* New York: Snow Lion.

Scientific American. November 2014.

Schrödinger, Erwin. 1958. *Mind and Matter.* New York: Cambridge Press.

Shantideva. 1997. *Guide to the Bodhisattva's Way of Life* (translated by B. Alan and Vesna Wallace. New York: Snow Lion.

Sheng, Chuan, Ed. *Exploring Buddhism and Science.* Singapore: Buddhist College of Singapore.

Siegel, Ronald D. 2013. *Mindfulness and Psychotherapy, Second Edition.* New York: Guilford Press.

Sogyal Rinpoche. 1992. *The Tibetan Book of Living and Dying.* San Francisco: Harper.

Surya Das, Lama. 1992. *Awakening the Buddha Within.* New York: Broadway.

Suzuki Roshi. 1970. *Zen Mind, Beginner's Mind.* New York: Weatherhill.

Thanissaro Bhikkhu. 2015. *The Karma of Mindfulness.* Valley Center, CA: Metta Forest Monastery

Thich Nhat Hanh. 2001. *Miracle of Mindfulness.* New York: Beacon Press.

Wallace, B. Alan. 2007. *Contemplative Science.* New York: Columbia Univ. Press.

_____. 2009. *Mind in the Balance: Meditation in Science, Buddhism, and Christianity.* New York: Columbia Univ. Press.

_____. 2012. *Meditations of a Buddhist Skeptic.* New York: Columbia Univ. Press.

Wilber, Ken. 2017. *The Religion of the Future.* Boston: Shambhala.

_____. 2006. *Integral Spirituality.* Boston: Shambhala.

www.ingramcontent.com/pod-product-compliance
Lightning Source LLC
Chambersburg PA
CBHW021059090426
42738CB00006B/422

9 781951 805432